FACES I HAVE SEEN

FACES I HAVE SEEN

a memoir of murder

VOLUME I

by

Ted Johnson

Lulu, Inc.
(Rev. ed.)

Revised edition, August 2010.

Edited by
Bradford Tolleson

Designed by
Modern Matter | A.J. Favors

Photography
Sheila Pree Bright

Typefaces
League Gothic made by The League of Moveable Type , Calson 540 designed by William Caslon I, and Gill Sans designed by Eric Gill.

Published by
Lulu, Inc.

Special thanks to: Kathryn Carrington, an author, grandmother and friend for her insight, understanding and instruction. Karen Porter who read my stories after she put her kids to bed and shared them with her husband, the positive feedback was appreciated. Afi Scope, my friend, my conscious that encouraged me to look at the other side of things.

ISBN 978-0-557-58417-8

To Mother, my dearest love, that taught me perseverance but cautioned me with patience.

CONTENTS

INTRODUCTION

* * *

This collection of short stories started out as my personal diary. My work became very stressful and I needed to find a release, so I began to write. While writing, I found myself evolving through an entire range of emotions including love, anger, and being judgmental of people. I was astonished by the ease of which people can exploit and inflict inhumane acts to one another. I also found significant parallels between the people that I had represented in murder cases and the people I knew as a child. As of the time of my first story, five of my cousins had been convicted of murder. My cousins were also my friends. We were raised that way. So, when I told someone that they did not want me to call my cousins, for those that knew me, that threat had real meaning.

Writing these stories has allowed me to grow in a much more spiritual way, which was very difficult. I think in the face of constant adversity, it's easy for one to become cynical, and view the glass as half empty as opposed to half full. So, in light of being reared by a father who was emotionally cold and stuck in time, and a mother who stayed with him for the welfare of her seven kids, I know what it means to sacrifice, by observing her suffer.

If an ex-girlfriend hadn't secreted herself and read my stories, I don't think I would've shared them. She, however, insisted. She felt these stories, at a minimum, could be entertaining to someone and relevant to a society of people who want to know how I think and how do my job from day to day.

At first, I refused because of my use of the ugliest of all words — the "N" word — that was used sparingly throughout some of the stories. This is a word that I, like most African Americans, detest on all levels. We acknowledge it is a rare word that when spoken it reaches to cause injury into the inner most part of our spirit with its sharp rusty blade — and it hurts. It's amazing how powerful we have allowed the word to become. My father once told me that if I quit because someone called me the "N" word, he would beat me. He reasoned that's what they wanted me to do.

Perhaps I could have removed the "N" word from my stories, but I feel it would have compromised the emotional authenticity of how I felt when the story was written. Besides, I thought that if I made reference to my mother in an embarrassing light, folks I don't know who are offended by my use of the "N" word might one day forgive me.

The title of the book comes from the sheer number of people I have represented in murder cases — faces of all different types, ages, sizes, races, and socioeconomic status — both male and female. Most of these people, in my representation of them, became a part of my life, and some I come to admire, if not love.

I chose this picture of me on the front porch of my childhood home. Please notice the holes in porch near my right foot. This is the only baby picture of me that exists. I had to step around this hole in the porch until I was at least 10, when my father actually fixed it. I had four older brothers who could have easily fixed the porch, but out of respect or fear of my father, they dared not.

Thus, I grew up dodging and avoiding holes in the pavement my whole life. Whether in concerns of love, life, or work, I've learned to identify the hole in the matter and move past it. The lady friend who secretly read my stories told me her family was afraid to meet me because of my status as a lawyer. Seemingly, they viewed themselves as simple working people. She laughed at their fears and told them I grew up drinking Kool-Aid out of mason jars and I grew up with holes in my porch. She told them not to be fooled by my suit. Funny, after her disclosure, her family accepted me. As tragic as these stories are, I ask you not to forget to laugh. At times, laughter is what keeps me from crying.

Chapter 1

Resolve

STRANGE FRUIT

"Southern trees bear a strange fruit blood on the leaves and blood on the roots...black bodies swinging in the southern breeze...strange fruit hanging from the poplar tree."

— Billie Holiday

My father started weaning me off of cartoons by the time I was seven years old. Like most seven year olds, cartoons were my thing. I loved cartoons and model airplanes. Like most kids, I always wanted to fly, but my father thought that at seven, I had had my fill of kid stuff. See, when my father was seven years old, his mother had died. His older brother had moved away and his father remarried a woman who had her own kids. At seven, my father was helping out in the cotton fields of Mississippi and was forbidden to go to school. He was needed in the fields. Feeling young and helpless, he could do nothing to stop his stepbrother from fucking his older sister. Feeling orphaned, he felt like he had gotten the last of everything. Forbidden to dream, my father's hope for life was replaced with his bitterness.

Thus, I grew up as the kid who was told that "I wasn't shit" because I could not hold the table lamp steady as my father fucked up mother's new sink trying to install it himself without the proper tools. Father was too cheap to just buy a flashlight. I was the kid who was called "a goddamn fool" if I thought someone would give me a scholarship or free education if I played basketball for their university. I was the kid whose father refused to give me, in his words, "a goddamn dime" if I quit my job to go to law school, as if school was for those who were less than a man or just for white folks. All my life, I had to learn how to wrap my immature and sensitive mind around understanding a man with a plantation mentality.

My father was reunited with his brother after nearly 30 years separation. One of his sisters had enlisted the help of the Red Cross and they found my Uncle Ed in Houston, Texas. I was told that my uncle had done some time for killing Mary's (his future wife's) then husband. Aunt Mary eventually explained to my father what sending me to college meant to her and for me to attend the very institution in Houston where she washed the sheets; even better, that the institution would pay for me to go there. As a young woman, she recalled that black folks and women weren't allowed to attend the institute. For her, she believed that me going there was a sign that things had come full circle.

For the longest, I thought that my father carried a gun with him everywhere he went because of his feeling of helplessness and abandonment as a child. I thought that his need to carry a gun everyday would have ended after he was reunited with his brother. But, I later learned that one had nothing to do with the other. And because of such, I long had the curiosity of the relationship between men and their sons, even as old as I am and with as many experiences as I've had. I guess the negative relationship I had with my own father pushed me to observe and seek out positive ones. I love women, but I can't explain my fascination with the camaraderie men have among each other.

On November 20, 1996 at 9am,
Madam Clerk: Your Honor, we call the case of the State of Georgia v. Fred Floyd, charged with murder.
Judge: Mr. Floyd, how do you plead?
Response: Not guilty, Judge.
Judge: Mr. Johnson what is your announcement?
Response: Ready for trial judge.
Judge: Madam Clerk, where is my jury?
Response: We are bringing them in now Judge.

When I first met Floyd, he was behind that wire mesh steel partition in the visitation booth at the county jail. The mesh made it so that you could only see a silhouette of your client and eye contact was virtually impossible. The visitation room only allowed us to communicate with the client without really seeing his facial expressions when we talked. During our first conversation, Floyd told me how he had found God.

Floyd would address me like he was in the military and I was his superior officer. I would say, "Floyd, how are you doing today?" and he would respond, "Fine, sir. Yes sir." Of course, Floyd, having found God in jail and his militaristic attitude, brought out my cynicism. It seems that all of my clients, after they have killed and raped someone, find Jesus out at the jail.

Based on how Floyd addressed me, I knew he had spent some jail time in one of those military boot camps for young offenders. At those camps, the inmates are instructed to address their superiors as if they are in fact in the armed forces. The idea behind the camp is to teach the boys discipline. Still, I wasn't impressed with Floyd's attempt to address me in such a way. I knew that Floyd was accused of killing his best friend because they argued over whom they were going to rob.

Seemingly, Floyd shot his friend in the face and in the ass

during their argument. Floyd then wrapped his friend up in a bed sheet and tied him up with a telephone cord. Thereafter, under the cover of night, Floyd dumped his body out of a second story window and dragged it underneath the crawl space of the shelter. Floyd then returned to his bedroom and cleaned up the blood. The body was recovered weeks later after the neighbors complained of the horrible stench coming from underneath the shelter.

After hiding his friend's body, Floyd fled to the suburbs and hung out with an old friend, Jason. Floyd and Jason were old partners in crime back in South Georgia. Jason was now a budding drug dealer and had his own drug crew. Floyd wanted to be a part of the crew, but Jason's crew was lukewarm at best toward Floyd. It was learned that there was some jealousy between Floyd and the other members of the crew. Like children, everyone wanted to be worthy of Jason's attention. Floyd, sensing the jealousy, told me that he didn't try to force himself on the crew.

Shortly after Floyd joined the crew, they robbed and killed a guy from Philly. The guy was looking to buy a kilo of cocaine before he was killed. Jason and his crew did not know what to do after they killed the guy. They were okay with just bleaching the scene. Floyd then volunteered to assist with the cleanup of the crime scene. He told the crew that he had been through this before. So Floyd had the crew to pull up the carpeting and the floor underneath the carpet to make sure that they got rid of all evidence of blood. Floyd went on to tell everybody that ammonia itself was not strong enough to get rid of the blood. It came to be that Floyd was arrested with Jason's crew for this murder before the police paid closer attention to the death of his friend.

I met Floyd's father, Reverend Clay, early on in the case. He would stop by my office and tried to provide information as best he could. Reverend Clay was a true missionary. He ran a couple of shelters in Atlanta; one for women and children, and the other for men. He also published a homeless newspaper for the residents to pass out in exchange for donations. A humble man, the shelters were his life's work and what he lived for. Reverend Clay told me how he tried to involve Floyd in his homeless ministry. He told me that if he did not insist that Floyd help out, he wouldn't. Floyd was staying with him at the men's shelter at the time he shot his friend. Reverend Clay told me that the shelters survived off of donations and grants. It was, indeed, bad news that a murder occurred at the shelter and Reverend Clay's own son was the only suspect.

Reverend Clay told me that Floyd had come to live with him after he was released from the prison boot camp for young offenders. He was divorced from Floyd's mom. I noted that he was not much younger than my own dad. However, Reverend Clay, in spite of everything, was a visionary that tried to help others. After meeting with him, I was convinced that he made me a better person. Yet, I wondered how Floyd fell so far from the tree and how it came to pass that he would lynch his own friend.

The victim had been shot twice. However, maggots had eaten the victim's brain matter and eyes, and the body was badly decomposed. Also, the chest cavity and stomach had been eaten out by maggots. The smell of the body was so nauseating; the medical examiner stated that after she observed a defect in the victim's jaw, she concluded that the shot to the face killed the victim. The second bullet was found lying in the victim's body bag. The medical examiner could not determine the path of the bullets because the victim's body was eaten up.

The day before trial, the astute prosecutor had the medical examiner examine the victim's clothing. Initially, the medical examiner had failed to do this. Upon examination of the victim's clothes, an entry wound was found in the buttocks area of the victim's sweatpants. That hole matched a hole in the victim's underwear. The only conclusion was that the two bullet fragments found in the victim's body bag were from the injury to the face and the other from the injury to the buttocks. The state surmised that the victim had tried to run from Floyd when he was shot in the buttocks. Then Floyd stood over the victim and shot him in the face.

So, here we are at trial. Floyd's dilemma was real and posed difficult questions and even more difficult answers. I told Floyd that to assert self-defense is difficult because the victim was shot in the buttocks. If the victim was first shot in the face, then there was no need to shoot him a second time in the buttocks. If the victim was first shot in the buttocks, why shoot him in the face unless you meant to kill him? On the other hand, if the shooting was an accident, why was it necessary to shoot him twice?

Floyd had told police on two occasions that he didn't know where the victim was. Floyd told police that he was looking for the victim because he owed him $20. Floyd then told police that the victim was avoiding him.

Floyd's case remained opened for two years, but I knew the trial was going to be over as soon as it began. The victim's mother was probably the state's first witness. I still dream about her and her pain. She wore her pain on her face. You could see her pain in her forehead and just underneath her eyes. She testified that after her son was missing for several days, she approached Floyd and asked for his help. She told the jury how Floyd would just play dumb like he didn't know anything. She stated that when she went back a second and third time, he played like he wasn't at home but she knew he was. The last time she approached Floyd, she told him, "Just tell me where he is. I won't tell the police anything. Just help me. I just want to bury him. I just want to sleep." She told the jury how Floyd just closed the door in her face. The jury cried. Quietly, I cried too.

Floyd told me that from time to time, he would go down to where he hid his friend and ask him, "What should I do?" He would ask his friend to pray for him and begged for his forgiveness. I asked him how he was able to deal with the smell. Floyd told me he just did. Guilty on all counts, the jury read its verdict without hesitation.

Floyd's mother told me that she should have never allowed Floyd to stay with his father, Reverend Clay. I cut her short. I told her that people are so quick to blame each other for the evil deeds of their children. I told her that Reverend Clay was a good man. There was no one to blame for Floyd's behavior and choices. I told her that Floyd was just a piece of strange fruit that fell from a poplar tree.

Sentence: Life in prison.

PEOPLE CHANGE

Mr. Rufus told Fifty Cents if he kept playing with him that he would kill him. Fifty Cents told Mr. Rufus that he wasn't "gon do shit" cause he wasn't on the goddamn property. Fifty Cents told Mr. Rufus that he acted as if the Lodge was his and that it wasn't. He was just a nigga' for the white folks that owned it. Mr. Rufus dropped Fifty Cents right there across the street from the Lodge, a shotgun blast to the face. You could see the birdseed pellets in Fifty Cents' neck and head area. They looked like peanuts stacked on top of each other inside of Fifty Cents' head.

I first met Mr. Rufus when Candy Man was busted for trafficking in cocaine over at the Lodge off of Fulton Industrial Boulevard, about 30 minutes west of Atlanta. Whatever vice you have — drugs, whores, boys, etcetera — you can get it off of Fulton Industrial Boulevard. The street is littered with truck stops, day motels and liquor spots.

Mr. Rufus showed me around the Lodge. The Lodge was really a trap for the dope boys to work out of. The whores, tricks, and homeless folks were the main customers. Candy Man gave me a 1972 drop-top Cutlass and $10,000 to represent him. When he saw the whites of the juror's eyes and realized that his cousin had turned state's evidence against him, Candy Man pled guilty to a reduced charge of possession of cocaine.

Mr. Rufus then hired me to represent his stepson, Prince. Prince was accused of fucking a runaway teenager hanging around the Lodge. Prince was barely grown himself. However, in hindsight, Prince may have saved the teenager from a life of prostitution. If Prince wasn't fucking her, someone else may have turned her into a whore. The folks at the Lodge dared not to confront Prince about the new pussy because of his connection to Mr. Rufus.

I got Prince off with a slap on the wrist. Mr. Rufus and his old lady Ms. Cathleen, Prince's mother, thought that I could walk on water because they knew Prince was fucking that runaway girl on the regular.

Everybody that hung out near the Lodge knew that Mr. Rufus was an old school, country pimp with a lot of insecurities. Country pimps are oft paranoid because they think that you're trying to play on their ignorance. They can barely read and women are more of a commodity than a love interest. I guess the same thing can be said for all pimps. It's just that country pimps are easily agitated and violent to compensate for their lack of coolness like citified pimps. Moreover, Mr. Rufus was from that generation of folks that if they told you that they would kill you, they meant it.

Mr. Rufus and Ms. Cathleen were people that lived on the fringes of society. They were the gatekeepers of society's crack heads, pimps, players, and whores. They claimed that Mr. Rufus would snitch out the dope boys to police because they'd cut into his drug business. Mr. Rufus was the security for the Lodge and Ms. Cathleen was the manager. At first, they felt more comfortable with the people that lived in the Lodge than they did with me.

I guess they could control the tenants, who were a step away from being homeless and oftentimes in need of a hit of crack. After a while, I was like their connection to the outside world, the world of squares and closet freaks. I think they knew that I had a purpose for them. I became their lawyer.

Neither Mr. Rufus nor Ms. Cathleen was academically educated, but both had PhDs in street life. They shunned away from life in the mainstream, almost scared to venture out. Dinner at the Pancake House was a significant outing. The Pancake House was considered uptown for them. Whatever their shortcomings and social incompetence, I knew these people and they knew me. I was raised around the Mr. Rufus' and Ms. Cathleen's of the world. And they knew this about me, so they trusted me and considered me family.

I know that I, like most people, attach myself to anything that's familiar to me. Living in a strange land, the South has benefited me tremendously. However, I do find it odd that there are people in America who will never accept me or my birth. Every chance they get, they remind me of it no matter how hard I try to fit in or reassure them that I'm okay, I'm the good one.

Still, Charity, one of my ancestors, lays in my family burial plot in Forrest, Mississippi. She lived and died in the days of Lincoln. Some would say as she should, that I'm more American than most. Charity would say that my life in America had been paid for.

It didn't take the jury a long time to convict Mr. Rufus. A federal cop happened upon the scene on his drive home from work. He observed Mr. Rufus standing over Fifty Cents yelling, "I told your ass to stop fucking with me." He described to the jury how he observed the 50-something black male with a bald head and medium brown complexion flee from the scene. The cop further stated that as he pulled closer to the scene, he observed how Fifty Cents' body was sprawled out in the middle of the road. The officer even described how folks from the shadows picked up the shotgun Mr. Rufus had used and carried it from the scene.

My defense was that the officer was mistaken, that he did not see Mr. Rufus because Mr. Rufus was in the country and not at the Lodge. I accused the officer of being in the area to buy some pussy. You know, I was looking for a Perry Mason moment when as a lawyer you have nothing significant to say about the facts of the case, you take personal shots at the witness. It didn't work. The state pulled Mr. Rufus' cell phone records and it showed that around the time of the murder, his phone was bouncing off the cell phone tower at the Lodge or one that was close to it. He wasn't in the damn country.

I was proud of Mr. Rufus because we had practiced his testimony for months. I had kept Mr. Rufus out of jail on bond for months before his trial. He had even managed to get a job at a chicken factory in the country near Augusta, Georgia. Mr. Rufus told the jury how he saved Fifty Cents' life when someone doused him in gasoline and set him on fire. Mr. Rufus placed a blanket around the inferno that was Fifty Cents and smothered the blaze. On another occasion, when some Mexican drug dealers came over to the property to kill Fifty Cents because he had robbed one of their crew members looking to buy some pussy, Mr. Rufus made Fifty Cents give the money back.

Notwithstanding, the fact he held a gun on Fifty Cents to get him to comply, either the Mexicans were gon' kill Fifty or Mr. Rufus was. The jury didn't buy anything Mr. Rufus had to say. During a recess, I asked Mr. Rufus why he let Fifty Cents make him so upset. Mr. Rufus said that he was just a pest. But people can change, especially if they live long enough. I'm glad I didn't know Mr. Rufus when I was younger.

My brother Harvey changed his name to Muhammad. But, like my cousin Cliff, he was a citified pimp and a hustler. His friends were just regular old Mississippi Niggas' just like him. They would talk shit to him about going back to Africa and asked how could he live without pork. Kevin and I would stand outside my uncle's bar and wait for Harvey right there on Meridian Street.

When Harvey showed up, we'd ask him for money. If he refused, we'd begin to call him all kinds of motherfuckers around his whores and friends. I'd tell him, "You ain't no goddamn Muhammad," and how I was going to beat his ass if he called himself Muhammad again. He would tell us if we called him Harvey, we would have hell to pay. This went on until either Harvey gave in and paid us or he'd catch us and beat the shit out us. Oh yeah, we'd cry, but we would wipe away the tears and post right back up in the same spot and commence to calling him Harvey. To his amazement, we could take the ass whipping. Eventually he would give in and pay us because we were bad for business.

I ran the same game on my cousin Cliff, the citified pimp. And he had some of the most beautiful women I had ever seen. Even though I was just 10 years old, I would flirt with them. I just wanted them to touch my dirty little face with their soft hands. I remember how nice they would smell. At 10, I didn't know the difference between perfume and pussy. I just remember the smell and I liked it. I remember how I would hang out at Cliff's spot across from the bus station to get a glimpse of his whores.

When Cliff learned that he couldn't chase me away, he would just give me money and I would leave. Back then, a dollar could buy you a meal at White Castle and leave enough left over to buy a chips and a coke for later that night. Cliff was one of the first people I saw with a Mercedes that didn't have a regular job. At the time, his cashmere evening jackets were something I only saw white men wear on the Ed Sullivan or Nat King Cole Shows.

Yes, I was a pest. I am sure Harvey and Cliff felt the same way about me as Mr. Rufus did about Fifty Cents, but people can change, especially if they live long enough.

Sentence: Life in prison.

EVERYDAY PEOPLE

Mr. George told me that he had met his wife, Grace, when he was five years old. They were neighbors. He told me that Grace was his first friend. They had been married for over 30 years with three adult kids, a dream house and a step away from retirement before he killed her.

As a child, Mr. George represented every man I had ever known in my life. He was a Southerner — proud and hardworking — he loved to drink and loved pussy.

In my neighborhood, your manhood was tied into who you were fucking, had fucked and who you were about to fuck. This was so even with the church dudes. It was just the way it was, even including my own father, which was part of the reason why I resented him so. Daddy never tried to hide his affairs, and every woman was fair game. At one time, Daddy and his own nephews were all fucking the same lady. One of the nephews even had a child with the woman.

Mr. George was from a single-parent home without a father. Since he was the only boy, he had to work and barely went to school. Mr. George worked early in his life and all of his life. As he got older, he played a little semi-pro football with his 6'3" frame, broad shoulders and 260 pounds all steel. He was a good athlete. Mr. George sported a Marlboro man mustache that didn't quite come to his chin and he was proud of his light brown complexion. With all of his physical attributes, Mr. George was considered a pretty boy. But, make no mistake about it, he was all man.

In the seventies and early eighties, his good looks won him bit roles in a few football movies. Rightfully, Mr. George was proud of this, however small the part was. I also noticed that Mr. George was rather materialistic for a man. He really liked nice things; Cadillacs, jewelry, clothes and such. I didn't hold it against him since I realized that Mr. George's childhood was rough. I mean, he never had shit and the shit he was able to accumulate in his adult life was important to him. Mr. George wanted name brand shit and wanted you to know that he had it or could get it if he wanted.

Moreover, as much as Mr. George was like every man I knew, he, too, enjoyed the pleasure of 30-something year-old pussy. It's just something about a 50-year-old man and 30-something year-old pussy that convinces him he needs to have a taste of it.

Being in my forties, I don't have the same compulsion for 20-something year-old pussy as the 50-year-olds have for the 30-something stuff. To make rhyme or reason out of this would be foolish. One can only surmise that the 50-year-olds may have the 40-something pussy at home and it has become worn and tired, common. On the contrary, the 20-something may remind him so of a daughter or niece. The pussy would be too tender or kind of tight and perhaps overly emotional.

But, the 50-year-old convinces himself that the 30-year-old pussy is just right. See, it gets just wet, loose and deep enough for thorough enjoyment. At 30-something, a woman is inclined to have been around the block a few times. She is more often than not in tune to her sexuality and she can tell you how she likes to be fucked or loved, as it were.

Mr. George said that that 30-year-old pussy will make a grown man's toes tingle. It'll make you spend all of your money before you go home only to start a fight with your wife, so you can get out and hit it again, if you're able you know; if you can get it up. We laughed.

Such were the southern men that I knew growing up in the Midwest. They would spend their last dollar on some 30-year-old pussy, even if it meant borrowing from friends at quarter on the dollar to buy some more.

During his 30 year marriage, Mr. George said that he put his wife through college while he worked at the railroad. I asked Mr. George if his wife ever stopped working while she was in school. He told me, "Hell naw." In Mr. George's mind, the fact that he let his wife go to school without quitting her job with the phone company was nice of him. See, he didn't have to let her go, but he did. This was the misogynistic thinking of not only Mr. George, but of my father.

Women, much like children, could do nothing without permission from the man of the house. After finishing school, Grace rose through the ranks of Corporate America.

Eventually, Grace began to make more money than Mr. George and he would use this against her. He would use it as his excuse or as a reason to beat her and go fuck around. He told me that sometimes he had to remind her of where she came from and who he was. Mr. George had to remind Grace of her indentured servitude status as if she thought that she could truly grow and evolve without him. My own mother could have told her that that would never happen.

But like any other young couple, they struggled.

However, after nearly 30 years of working at the phone and railroad companies, they got on their feet. And like the rest of the world, they sought for and obtained the American dream — their dream home. For the most part, on the outside, they appeared to be a happy couple. But as in every home, the skeletons in the dark unlit closet were many, deep, and ugly.

Lil Junior, Mr. George's only son, resembled his father but was not as big or tall. My initial impression of him was that he wanted to help his dad out but did not want to lie for him. He made it clear to me that he was not going to do anything that would reflect badly on his mother. Lil Junior was a momma's boy.

Lil Junior was married to a physician and they lived in Carolina. Mr. George told me how he had to talk to Lil Junior about jumping on his wife. Indeed, the fruit doesn't fall too far.

Understandably, Lil Junior was hesitant to talk to me about what we needed for him to do and say in Mr. George's defense. When I brought up the subject, Lil Junior interrupted me and said that every weekend for as long as he could remember up until he was about 18 years old, his dad would come home from work, wash his car, change clothes, start a fight with his mother, beat her up, and then leave for the weekend. Mr. George would then return on Sunday evening, beat Grace again because either he didn't like what she had cooked for Sunday dinner; or they didn't save him the big piece of chicken; or the food wasn't warm enough when he got home.

When he was 18, Lil Junior intervened in one of their arguments. When Mr. George chased him out of the house and fired a shotgun at him, Lil Junior told me that was the last time he lived with his parents.

Lil Junior's story reminded me of a conversation that I had with my oldest brother, who is actually old enough to be my father. I told him once that I was happy that I did not grow up in a family where my father would beat my mother. My brother told me the only reason that I didn't see it was because now that my other brothers were all grown, Rock, my father's nickname, would have to kill all of us. He figured that was too much killing to get away with.

He also shared with me his childhood experience of my mother catching my father with one of his girlfriends. Upset because she caught him, my father dragged my mother by her hair down the street. My brother's point was I wasn't born when he'd beat Mother and they were too old and tired to have been fighting when I grew up. I guess that's why I didn't march with my classmates at my own high school, college, or law school graduations. I knew that my parents were too tired to show up. My oldest brother died a couple of years ago. He was in his late sixties.

Even upon hearing Lil Junior's story, I thought about how my father beat my brother in the head with a hammer. My brother was accused of allowing his friends to hide some stolen cases of Coca-Colas in our shed. I was only six years old when my dad had hid himself underneath my brother's bed and waited for him to come home. When my brother made it home, my father came from underneath the bed with the hammer in one hand and his pistol in the other. As they struggled, my brother pleaded with him to calm down. Rock told my brother to choose his medicine.

My father struck my brother so hard in the head with that hammer, the blow caused a subdural hematoma around his head. My brother's blood splattered on my face and clothes. I should have been in preschool during this episode, but I had been kicked out for fighting my teacher. She had tried to force me to go swimming and I didn't want to get into the water. So I kicked her in the shins while wearing my steel toe Buster Brown boots.

My brother was a high school senior and only 18 years old when my father attacked him. At 30, a tumor was removed from my brother's head. At 35, my brother overdosed on some bad drugs. Today, I regret being kicked out of school on that day. I regret having witnessed my father's violent abuse of my brother.

Lil Junior told me the story of being shot at in the presence of his father, so I knew he wasn't lying or exaggerating. At first, Mr. George said nothing, but as soon as Lil Junior left us, Mr. George told me he didn't shoot directly at Lil Junior. He just shot in the air to scare him. I remembered Mr. George saying this to me as if he was somehow proud of his aim. Mr. George had this slow grin on his face. You know the grin that blurs the line of deviance, stupidity and retardation; the smile that the mirrored sunglasses-wearing cop gives you after he gives you a speeding ticket. Lil Junior told me that if his Daddy didn't plead guilty, he would tell this same story to the jury as he had already told the police.

Mr. George's oldest daughter, Missy, was about 32 years old. She was tall, but you could tell she had never done anything athletic in her life. Missy was bordering on obesity, but she had this beautiful mane of hair that fell to her shoulders and her caramel brown complexion helped her appearance out as well. To look at Missy, one would say she would be fine if she lost 100 pounds.

Missy had never accomplished anything in her life through her own efforts. At least, Lil Junior was in the real estate game and his baby girl was in college. Missy, on the other hand, could not keep a job past a year. Missy had quit the military and college. Her parents rented her an apartment just to get her fat ass out of the house. However, Missy did have a boyfriend, Officer Wayne, of the Atlanta Police Department. Seemingly, the death of Grace was the opportunity of a lifetime for Missy. She had moved into the estate while it was still a crime scene. Missy even slept in the same bed and room where her mother had just died minutes ago.

None of this mattered to Missy, neither her mom's drying blood on the white Berber carpet nor her dad, the alleged murderer. Perhaps, this was just Missy's way of grieving. Naw, Missy just wanted to make sure that she got the house before Lil Junior did.

Missy was able to convince Mr. George in a matter of days to deed the house over to her and he did, along with all of the insurance policy proceeds. Imagine living in an apartment one month and both parents refusing to pay your rent, and the very next month, you're the sole owner of this 5,000 square-foot home on 13 acres and a five-car garage. Even more, you are now the trustee of tens of thousands of dollars in insurance money. Missy literally had no time to grieve for either parent.

Officer Wayne was a nice enough guy, but it was apparent that he never had a decent enough looking woman and Missy was the best that he could do. Officer Wayne, however, unlike me, loved Mr.

George. Officer Wayne told me that Mr. George had been good to him and a father figure. See, Officer Wayne came round when Mr. George either wasn't beating Grace as much or had just mellowed out some with age.

I ran into Officer Wayne downtown after I was able to get Mr. George out of jail on bond. Officer Wayne told me that perhaps my read of Missy was a bit over the top. Officer Wayne claimed that Missy harbored a lot of resentment toward her parents. Missy claimed that Mr. George had molested her as a teenager. After Missy told her mother, she felt like her mother didn't believe her and did nothing about it.

Besides, Missy had allowed Mr. George to live in the basement of his house while out on bond and she hired me. Without any evidence to counter or contradict Missy, I believed Mr. George when he denied molesting Missy. I thought to myself that my father was a womanizer, but he never fucked my sisters.

In my mind, Missy was just a straight up loser and she was just as materialistic as her father — she had no conscience. I'd ask myself how she could sleep in the bedroom where her mother's blood saturated and stained the floor. In my mind, how strange and sick it was that Missy could sleep in her mother's bed. I wondered if Missy could feel her mother's spirit in that room; if Missy could feel her mother's pain, rage, and jealousy; or did it just anger Missy that as twisted as her father was, her mother still loved him more than she loved her. Thirty years of marriage and Mr. George and Grace never separated. Never did it cross my mind that perhaps it was the behavior of a little girl that had been molested by her father and her mother didn't believe her.

No one expected me to get Mr. George out of jail on bond. I argued to the judge that Mr. George had no real criminal record and besides, this was simply a domestic violence case. Hence, Mr. George was only a threat to his wife and she's now dead. Missy told the judge that she was afraid of her father. Everyone knew she was lying. Missy just didn't want Mr. George home. See, she had already moved in her boyfriend, Officer Wayne. The judge bought my bullshit argument and let him out.

After Mr. George was released on bond, he courted me like I was his newfound friend and son. I admittedly played into it, like he was the father I had long resented. But, now, I have an opportunity to do something for him. To show him who and what I had become, to seek the approval and validation I thought that daddy owed me.

To the contrary, when I told my father that I had gotten a scholarship to play ball at a prestigious university in Texas, he told me to get school off my mind because they couldn't afford to pay for it. Once I explained to him what a scholarship was, he told me I was a damn fool if I thought someone was going to pay my way through school to play a kid's game. When I began to excel on that level, he told me that if I made it big, that I was going to take care of him if I wanted to or not. I refused to play professional ball overseas, for some reason.

After my graduation, I got a job with the City of Houston in the legal department. I worked there two years before I decided to go to law school. After I got accepted into law school, I called home to share the good news. My father told me that I had been to school long enough and that I needed to keep my job. When I disagreed with him, he told me that if I quit my job not to ask him for a dime.

I started law school the year after my brother overdosed. Before I could ask him for anything, my father died. I was a second year law student. So here I am with Mr. George still trying to forge a relationship with my dad, nearly 10 years after his death. Mr. George took me to expensive steakhouses and we'd talk about all of the pussy each other was getting. I had never been to dinner with my dad or engaged him in an adult conversation before he died. Honestly, I can't say that I wanted to.

Inevitably, Mr. George would blame his own wife for her death. He'd say, "She knew I was a ho when she married me and she also knew that I would whip her ass if she tried me." I guess subconsciously, I was affirming Mr. George's logic because each time we were together, her blame became easier for him to say until I accepted his comments as the truth.

The truth that I'm speaking of is not the truth that distinguishes right from wrong. But that truth you find in an established fact like the truth of existence; the truth of what is or was in the present or past; the multiplicity truth of rationalizing the character flaws of greed, selfishness and intolerance; the truth that we hope that people will change; the smelly truth of living in my daddy's house and how he treated my mother. The singular truth of this is how it is and you can't do shit about it; the truth of knowing from experience.

On a summer's night in June, Mr. George had found some 30-year-old pussy. It didn't matter to Mr. George how unattractive the pussy was or that it seemed to smell. Being the addict that he was, when the pussy called Mr. George, he goes to get that pussy. In the past, there had been several affairs. Like my father, Mr. George didn't go too far to hide his indiscretions because he felt like he didn't have to.

On this summer's night, the pussy paged Mr. George. As always, Grace knew when Mr. George was fucking around. Mr. George went into the other room to return the page. After Mr. George got off the phone, Grace told Mr. George that she had made plans for them to eat dinner with friends. Mr. George chastised her for not telling him earlier and that he had made plans for himself. Besides, he had spent all morning and afternoon with her.

Mr. George then showers, dips himself in cologne and leaves the house. Mr. George told me that he saw the lights in his house go out as he drove down the driveway. He told me that he had doubled back to make sure that Grace was not following him. When he was sure that she was still inside, Mr. George went to get the pussy.

Mr. George told me that when he got to the pussy, he started to get the pussy ready. He told me the pussy liked cognac before fucking so they were working on their second drink, when someone knocked on the door. Pussy looked out the window and told Mr. George there was a woman outside with a gun in her hand. Mr.

George looked outside and saw that it was his wife. Mr. George told me that back in the day, he would have opened the door, beat her ass and sent her back home. I remembered when my father shot his girlfriend Ms. Nancy in the mouth right in our backyard.

Ms. Nancy had come over to confront my mother. Daddy told her as he put the gun in her mouth, "I told you if you came over here, I was going to shoot you in the mouth." As he pulled her head back by her hair, he pulled the trigger. I watched as Ms. Nancy grabbed her mouth and hit the ground. The bullet ricocheted off her teeth and jawbone before leaving her mouth. Luckily, Ms. Nancy lived. However, her face was permanently disfigured.

After the shooting, I remembered my parents sleeping in the same bed. In the following days, I remembered how hard it was to go to school with Ms. Nancy's kids. They were my friends. I felt ashamed of my fear when I saw them. I saw the confusion and indecision on their faces when they looked at me. They just lived a street over from us and we were all neighbors. Daddy was never arrested for shooting Ms. Nancy but that's another story.

So, I knew Mr. George wasn't bullshitting me when he told me this. I believed him because he was of the men that I have known my whole life. Mr. George said that he did not answer the door, he just watched her in silence through the peephole. When Grace returned to his car, she let the air out of his tires and then wrote on his windshield in red lipstick, "if you come home I will kill you" before she left in her truck.

After she left, Mr. George said he then got that 30-year-old pussy since he was there. He said he fucked her as much and long as he could. Mr. George recalled how all of that excitement made the pussy better than what it had been, and we laughed. He told me that he then checked on his car, when he saw Grace's message.

Mr. George returned to pussy and got some dish washing liquid and paper towels to clean off his windshield. He then let pussy read it before he wiped it clean. Mr. George then threw the paper towel on the ground (it was recovered by police the next day) and proceeded to a gas station to air up his tires.

After he aired up his tires, Mr. George then jumped in his Cadillac Seville and drove straight home. When he got there, he found that the gates to the house had been locked with a chain and padlock wrapped in duct tape. The gate and fence was about 10 feet high and was made of wrought iron. The fence surrounded the entire 13 acres around the house. Finding his remote to the gate didn't work, Mr. George, who was in his mid fifties, climbed over the 10-foot high gate.

As he got to the house, he peered through a window looking for Grace. He recalled that it was pitch dark inside the house except for the light from the television. Chairs had been placed underneath all the doors and the windows were all locked. The house was completely fortified. I asked Mr. George, "Why didn't you just leave?" My question angered him. He looked at me with disappointment before he replied, "This is my goddamn house and no one locks me out of my house."

I knew without him saying that he was going in to beat Grace's ass, that the first ass whipping was for following him over to pussy's and the second ass whipping was for locking him out of his goddamn house. It didn't matter to Mr. George or my father that they had been caught fucking around. Mr. George told me that it wasn't like it was his first time. She should have dealt with it better.

I told Mr. George that the story may come off a little better if he told the jury when he didn't see his wife anywhere in the house and he feared that she was about to harm herself. Mr. George said that's exactly how he felt since she was going through menopause and all. He needed to enter the house to see about her, to make sure she was all right, "a welfare check."

After several attempts to get Grace to open the door and repeatedly calling her name, Mr. George went to the back of the house. The back deck led to the master bedroom. The French doors had a chair underneath them, but as French doors are, they were rather flimsy. Mr. George kicked in the cute French doors and Grace emerged from the bedroom curtains. She had concealed herself in the floor-to-ceiling curtains with the two shot derringer he had bought for her to carry in her purse. Mr. George said he grabbed her arm and they wrestled over the gun, struggling in a dark house lit only by the television.

She knew that she was no match for Mr. George and she knew that he was going to whip her ass. I imagined that she was just as tired of getting her ass whipped as she was of him fucking around. A single shot was fired and the bullet literally struck Grace through the heart. Mr. George told me that when she fell to the floor, she was dead. He told me he went to the pantry and took out a fifth of cognac and drunk it before he called police, he just sat there and cried.

At trial, the prosecutor accused Mr. George of not having any remorse for what he had done to Grace and that he wanted her to die. To contradict this outrageous assertion, I played the 911 tape of Mr. George's call to police. On the 911 recording, through his tears and pain, you could hear Mr. George howling like a wolf at a full moon. In the courtroom, Mr. George cried and this time, I cried with him.

Seemingly, everything was gone for Mr. George and Grace. They both were months away from retirement, three adult kids, dream house, empty nesters — but still young enough to enjoy life. And it was all gone.

As expected, all three of Mr. George's kids testified for the state against their father. They spoke of the violence they witnessed all of their lives. Baby girl testified that when she got the call to come home from Missy, Missy only told her that "it's about Mommy." Baby girl then replied, "He finally did it." Missy replied, "Yes."

My father once said to me that I disliked him so much that if he were ever in trouble or in a fight, my brother Bill would jump right in and help. But I would have to think about it — if I'd help at all. I fought for you, Mr. George, not just because you paid me; but to prove you wrong, Daddy.

Sentence: Life in prison.

Chapter 2

Love

I WANT TO BE LOVED

When the jury returned to the courtroom, the judge instructed us to stand as the verdict was read. As I always do, I sighed and gasped for air. The Foreperson stated, "We, the jury, find the defendant as to count one murder, not guilty." There was a pause for just a second before everything hedged along in slow motion. "Count two: we, the jury, find the defendant guilty of felony murder." Sara turned and fell on me and sobbed openly. It felt so right, even though I was not supposed to have felt anything. She was a client.

You see, any remote intimate feelings for a client one way or another are considered taboo. I never violated that written rule, but there was the 25-year-old charged with battery after she got into a fight with her boyfriend. And, the sister of a victim in another murder case that looked me up after the first trial but she was not a client. Moreover, that was over 10 years ago.

It's pretty common for people to become attached to their therapist, teacher, doctor, or lawyer. This false sense of emotional attachment or obligation develops between people when they seek professional help premised on the notion that this professional is fighting for my rights, health, or some privilege they believe they're entitled to.

Sara was about 5'10," 145 pounds and very shapely. She had medium length hair that she wore as a natural Afro, crinkly and very stylish. I bought her two suits, a navy-blue pantsuit that hugged her body and a green business suit that showed off her shapely legs. Yes, Sara had some real calf muscles, not those chicken legs like most black women. I just couldn't believe that I had fallen for my client, the "dike," which meant I really fought for her. I mean I fight for all of my clients but I'm human, too. To me, Sara represented a future I could have with a woman that understood love.

Sara grew up in Brooklyn with drug-addicted divorced parents. Early in her life, Sara had bounced around between both parents as custody battles ensued. When her dad was out of prison, she'd live with him. Otherwise, she stayed with an aunt and her maternal grandmother. Luckily for Sara she had a grandmother. It was clear to me that any love that was constant in her young life came from her. Sara moved in with her grandmother when she was seven years old and stayed until her grandmother died when Sara was only 16.

Her grandmother had left a brownstone to Sara's mother and uncle, but living with the two proved to be too much for Sara. Sara's uncle would lock himself up in his room for days on end getting high on heroin. He was a Harvard dropout with a drug problem.

At some point, Sara's mother decided to become a "dike." She usually aligned herself with any woman who didn't mind paying the bills or getting high. Prior to trial, she only called me on two occasions. When I asked her to buy Sara some clothes, she had to get back to me. I wondered how bankrupt and impotent one must feel not to have given anything to one's child other than the gift of life or, in Sara's case, life's tortured suffering. In either instance, is the gift of life supposed to be enough? On everything, I need to believe there's more.

From the vulnerable age of 16, Sara was on her own. I respected

Sara because she was able to get her own apartment, continued to go to school, and graduated with her class. Sara even completed nearly two years of college, all of this while working at McDonald's and cutting hair on the side.

When I first met Sara, she was being held at the Fulton County Jail. Her head was shaved by choice and you could see a few little freckles in her reddish brown complexion. She had sincere almond eyes and a bashful girly smile. Sara's facial features were the only things that would give you any indication that Sara was a woman. She wore extremely baggie clothes to hide her shape. You could say that her clothes were her armor. Her voice was not particularly feminine and she even walked like a dude.

Fulton County Jail is in the heart of Atlanta and is just like any other jail — fucked up. Someone had the idea to paint the walls in the joint chocolate brown. This had the effect of making the place even more drab and morbid than what it was.

Even worse is to deal with some of the deputies over there that are wannabe police officers that couldn't pass the test. You should see them, especially the dude who walks around like a poor imitation of the Marlboro man with this cigar stub in the corner of his mouth.

This other dude that works the desk loves to nit pick with the attorneys when they come to visit with their clients. He may speak, he may not; he may ask for your credentials to start the process for the visit; he may just stand in front of you for a few seconds and say nothing, then he will walk away from you and make you wait unnecessarily for an additional 20 minutes while he's faking his ministerial duties behind the desk. However, when he's standing in front of you and you just give him your credentials, he may take them or he will tell you he can only do one thing at a time and make you wait. To me, it is always more frustrating when men act like bitches as opposed to dealing with men with bitch in them. The difference is all in the attitude.

Then there are the female deputies who will step to you with their asses on their shoulders. They may offer you some assistance in between their personal phone calls or conversation amongst themselves. You know, it's that DMV attitude when you're just trying to get your license.

Sara, as most clients, attempted to bullshit me straight out the gate. This didn't offend me since I'm used to dealing with bullshit clients anyway. My standard response to bullshit is that bullshit recognizes bullshit. Defense attorneys are professionally trained bullshitters. So if you give me a bullshit story, you'll have a bullshit defense. I try to make it clear that I won't allow myself to look like an idiot for anyone. And I won't, if I can help it, be caught with my dick in my hand because some client has given me a bullshit story. There's nothing worse than a judge that doesn't trust that you've done your homework before trial. They will treat you like you're invisible.

Usually, after my little spiel, I'll get up and leave the client in the booth for about a month or so before I visit with them again. If they continue to bullshit me, I'll get up and leave again for another month. By the next time I visit, they would have been in jail for so long that I get their full attention. Or at least, seemingly, they attempt to be more forthright with me, which is a good thing.

However, Sara came clean after my little sermon. Sara told me she had moved to Atlanta seeking a better life. After her grandmother died, Sara took up barbering as a teenager in New York. The neighborhood barber took her under his wings and began to teach her the craft of cutting hair. He was old enough to be her dad and he even had kids her age, but it didn't stop him from trying to fuck her.

Sara said she has dressed like a boy since fifth grade and has always liked girls. Personally, I think she became a dike because of what her mother exposed her to early on in her life. Feeling trapped because she didn't have a license to cut hair and the constant sexual harassment, Sara quit cutting hair and started selling drugs. Her father the jailbird, her uncle the dope fiend, and the barber were Sara's benchmark for what a man was. She never had a boyfriend or sex with a man.

To Sara, Atlanta represented a life away from the drugs and her skirt-chasing mother. While hustling, Sara had saved up enough money to catch the bus from Brooklyn. She was to stay with an old sweetheart who had moved here a year ago.

Sara explained that when she arrived to Atlanta, broke and without a job, the old sweetheart put her out within a few weeks. At that point, Sara found a little knife with a four-inch blade that she kept in her pocket. This was her only protection from the threat of being raped. Sara eventually found a job cutting hair in a shop downtown. The owner allowed her to work without a license. She lived in a shelter or day hotel above the shop.

Terry Weems and the victim worked in a restaurant next to the barbershop. The victim and Sara became acquaintances. Over time, Sara and Terry became lovers. This was Terry's first lesbian relationship. Sara thought she found someone who would take care of her. Terry was only 19 and obese with braided bleach blonde extensions. Terry was irritatingly silly and irresponsible. Personally, I thought Sara could do better. On the contrary, when it comes to affairs of the heart, who's to say what tickles one's toes and what doesn't? Within a few weeks, Terry and Sara pooled their monies and were able to get an apartment downtown.

Sara had been accused of stabbing the victim to death. She had given him 30 of her last 50 dollars to go to the store, and he never returned. The story goes that Sara and Terry drove around Atlanta until they found the victim in a crack den on the corner of Auburn Avenue and Piedmont Road. He had spent their money. Sara gave him one in the stomach with her knife and told him that "you better have my money the next time I see you." She and Terry then jumped back into Terry's car and drove away. The victim died walking to the hospital. A crack pipe was found right above his right hand and crack was found in his blood system. He was a 50-year-old man, a father, a brother, a male prostitute, and a crackhead. Two other crackheads and Terry were the only witnesses to the stabbing.

Sara told me that she and Terry did go looking for the dude but only to get her money back. She said they argued over the money and the victim just walked into the knife and died. Even as her lawyer, I'm thinking, "how does a motherfucker walk into a knife?" But it was important that I believe Sara if I was going to help her or at least come up with my own version of the story. "Oh, I almost forgot," Sara said. The dude apologized to her for walking into her knife. Yeah, okay, I had a lot of work to do.

I wanted to believe Sara's version so badly but I knew better. This was by far not my first stabbing case and I'm sure it won't be my last. As I continued to listen to Sara, I'm subconsciously thinking of how one knows one's dying after you've been stabbed. You are still conscious as your lungs fill up with blood. Your breaths get shorter and shorter as it becomes more difficult to breath. You are able to explain how you feel as the death process continues to inch it's way into total consumption of your lungs. Your stomach and chest begins to ache at the same time your vision becomes blurred. You are aware of the darkness as you step through the door of surrealism and death. After a few minutes, depending on your height, weight, and personal physical characteristics, you die.

As Sara continued to talk, I'm thinking that the knife had to go through this man's tough, rusty, crusty-ass skin and then through his compact abdominal muscles before it reached the internal organs. It had to pass through the internal organs before ultimately severing an artery in his back. Sadly, Sara's story sounded like a "three" to me (very odd).

I left Sara and went to the medical examiner's office. The morgue's office has come a long way. Back in the day, they'd put you in an office and you could hear someone's scalp being cut with the saw to pull their face down to check the brain for injuries. Today, they put you in a nice air-conditioned room with the slide photos of the decedent. They will even offer you a coke or coffee if they like you or if the appointment clerk does not have too much homework (she's in college).

The medical examiner walked out and greeted me. She was a rather frumpy woman with symbolic highlighted dreads. She was new to me; I had never worked with her before. Thus, I had no relationship with her whatsoever, damn.

Some medical examiners really take on the roll of the TV character, Quincy. They talk too much and make too many assumptions. I figured, however, there was some hope because she was a sister and so was the defendant.

She was a fellow forensic pathologist from I think somewhere in Chi-Town. Top shelf in terms of her academic credentials but rather uptight, kind of like she needed a cigarette or a good fuck. I guess she was as surprised as I was to see that we both were black. But you'll see that and all other types of professionals in Atlanta, unlike anywhere in America — The Black Mecca. Like so many others, Sara wanted to be around us and like many, she paid the cost.

Atlanta can be a friendly and down-to-earth place but it's rather cliquish. She's full of ideas, opportunities, and optimisms. However, as with anywhere else, it helps if you come to her with something. Don't get me wrong, many have come here with just a dream and made it. However, just like the bright lights of Hollywood and New York City, a number of souls become lost. And Atlanta, in her own nonchalant way, will just charge those lost souls to the game.

I was ready to lay the charm on the medical examiner in hopes that she would throw me a bone. It always helps when the medical examiner gives some information that's not in the autopsy report. But she saw me coming and played me straight. After telling the medical examiner Sara's version of the facts, I again tried to appeal to her empathy. Someone in her family had gotten into a fight and killed a man. As misogynistic and ignorant as it sounds, I thought that most "dikes" would rally behind such a notion. That angle didn't work and neither did the walking into the knife theory Sara had given me as an explanation.

The medical examiner stated that whoever stabbed this dude severed an artery in his spine. The dude was stabbed in the stomach, for Christ's sake. If anything, the medical examiner was telling me without saying it, that somebody stabbed the shit out of this dude and that was her story and she was sticking to it. Bitch.

I had to call Terry several times before she would even return my calls. Terry stood me up twice after I had reassured her that I would not drop a dime on her to the police. Terry was accused in a 17-count indictment for identity theft and fraud. Even if I wanted to drop a dime on Terry, it would only make Sara look bad by association, since they lived together when Terry's charges came down.

Terry had given a statement to police where she described the encounter between Sara and the victim as a little scuffle. After my conversation with the medical examiner, I knew that Terry's description of the scuffle had to grow into a fight between Sara and the victim. I thought easy enough, people that love each other help each other.

On the eve of trial, I had a telephone interview with Terry. This interview lasted for about an hour. Terry was all set to describe the little scuffle as a scuffle that escalated into a fight. I'm thinking that if Terry testified to this interpretation of facts, Sara walks. See, Terry was the only independent eyewitness that was not a crackhead. Terry was well spoken. She had worked in their family-owned business with the victim. I thought, great, Terry knows everyone involved, Sara and the victim.

After piecing together this case for trial, I thought Sara had found true love with Terry. I was genuinely happy for Sara because Sara thought she had what everyone else wanted; love. Surely, Terry would save her lover. At least Sara was confident that she would. I remembered telling Sara that Terry's on board. We made eye contact as if we were saying to each other, "I'll see you after this shit is over."

At trial, the theory of my defense went up in flames. I thought that most people would naturally empathize with a woman that's been taken advantage of by a man, particularly someone who was a crackhead and a thief. However, Terry described the victim as an okay guy with a drug problem. Seemingly, Terry's fear of the District Attorney outweighed her commitment to Sara.

I asked Terry would she describe the little scuffle between this man and Sara as a fight, and Terry replied no, she wouldn't. I then asked Terry if she and Sara shared an apartment together downtown. Terry would only admit that she would visit Sara at her apartment often but they did not live together. Finally, I asked Terry was she Sara's lover, and she replied "No," she only experimented with Sara and that they were not lovers.

After this, Sara's conviction was certain. Apparently, Terry was not ready to come out of the closet. She was not willing to come clean about her relationship with Sara at no cost to herself. Ironically, Sara's conviction was the price she had to pay for Terry's shame of being her lover. Hence, Peter was gone and no rooster crowed to prepare Sara for what was about to happen. At trial, Sara's mother never showed up and there were only a handful of spectators present. I don't think they were even interested in the case. They were just Court observers. Sara was alone. There were no pictures of Jesus in this state-owned building Sara could pray to. Her faith was just hanging in the balance.

The jury all but ignored Sara's description of how she struggled with the victim and how the victim grabbed her before she stabbed him with the little knife she had found. It didn't help when Sara explained how the New York Police told her to make the stabbing appear to be an accident. Sara had fled to New York after the stabbing and was arrested by NYPD several months later. Of course, the NYPD denied influencing Sara's statement. Perhaps, the jury may have felt that Sara lied once in her statement to the NYPD, she would lie again to save her life. I certainly would.

After the jury read their verdict, Sara sunk into my arms, sobbing and helpless. She tells me that the $30 the man ran off with was actually Terry's money. Being her lover, Sara went with her to get it back. She was Terry's savior and avenger. Terry was her girl and lover. Lovers take care of each other, right? What could I say but yes, lovers are supposed to take care of each other.

The most compelling human experience I ever had was to witness the completeness of love Sara had for Terry. The need to love sometimes outweighs the love one needs in return. In any given relationship, we can find ourselves wearing one hat or the other. So long as the quiet desperation of our existence is tolerable, we will introduce our significant others as our husband or wife suppressing whatever's underneath.

Like so many of us, Sara was accused and convicted of loving the wrong one. A few weeks ago, I bumped into a juror that was an assistant principal in the school system. He wanted my business card and told me I did an excellent job. I said well, not well enough. He replied, if her girlfriend wouldn't back her up how could we. I told him that I was out of cards.

Sentence: Life in prison.

LOVE FOR SALE

Dirty Bitch

At 48 years old, Millsap was only five years older than me, but it seemed like he had lived a lifetime. Millsap had a round face and he sported a short fro. Millsap had no upper teeth and he was crackhead skinny but with a beautiful muscular build. His mustache was unkempt and he was usually unshaven. In slavery days, his medium brown complexion would have given him certain privileges that a darkie like me would not have enjoyed. But, as it seemed, this beautiful brown complexion was wasted on him.

I won't soon forget that in the midst of his murder trial, in front the victim's friends and family, judge and jurors, Millsap still had the presence of mind to mug to the witness stand. In all of his ignorance, he remembered the walk.

I knew what it was as soon as I saw it. Some would say it's a black thing and some would say it's generational, it was something prevalent in the Zoot Suit 1940's but carried over through the 60's and 70's. But I still see it today in music videos, even in the streets where it was born. I remembered as a kid how my brother and I would imitate our older brothers' and cousins' walk. The walk had to be unique to you. You would be called out if you imitated someone else's walk. See, it was understood that the walk represented something about you, your stock in the world, your pretense, and your coolness.

The walk determined if others would even see you or speak to you. The walk was your first impression. Every time I see Denzel, I still see the walk, shoulders back, head slightly tilted back to the left or right. Your gait had to be smooth. See there was a limp or a shorter step one would make with his right leg so the left leg could catch up. It's like walking with a stutter, a walking impediment without a medical defect or reason.

Some brothers would never let the left leg lead. The left leg would always trail the right leg. You could go with a pigeon toe and a bowleg; you could go slew-footed or various other combinations, your arms slightly behind your body with a backward fist or open cuff-like position. The walk had several names — pimping, mugging or strutting.

I'm thinking to myself, this jury doesn't know anything about Millsap's first alleged killing of the white woman. He's on trial for this second murder and facing life in prison. But, in this brother's mind, he has instinctively reminded himself to remember that the good white folks on his jury must see his stupid ass pimp to the witness stand. My nigga.

Ms. Ruby was Millsap's older sister and was a sweet old Georgia peach. Like Millsap, she was not very well educated but extremely well mannered and humble. Even though she was old enough to be my mother, Ms. Ruby represented what one likes about the South. I bet all of the little white kids that she nursed still called after her in their adult life. Her spirit was soft and special. She was kind.

Her concern for Millsap was much like a parent's concern for their child. Ms. Ruby would call me time and time again until I just stopped answering her calls. I didn't get it at first, but after a few months it hit me. She was Millsap's' mother after their biological mother past away when Millsap was just a boy. I learned that

Millsap was the baby boy who never got his shit together when his mother died.

He was the youngest of five and they spoiled him. They spoiled him because they felt sorry for him. Millsap's siblings were all grown when they lost their mother and he was but a boy. They spoiled Millsap so that no one ever taught him how to try, work, or stand on his own.

So he became what he was; a semi-literate, drunk, crack-head that was a generation away in his mind from still calling white folks master. A slave to his alcohol/crack addiction and crippled by his own self-loathing, a nigga.

Ms. Ruby got so tired of calling me about going to visit Millsap. She tried to hire my buddy Walter but she couldn't afford him. I really didn't give a fuck, but it kind of made me shitty that it was Walter she tried to hire and not a stranger. But she didn't know.

My attitude toward Ms. Ruby changed when I first met her, a fragile lady in her sixties fighting brain cancer. I saw her sitting in her wheelchair in the corner of her modestly decorated living room. She was trying to show me favor by tugging at her head to straighten out her wig. I was flattered and moved that she cared. She was fighting for her life and she still cared enough about her younger brother to make sure he would be all right. It was clear to me that Ms. Ruby had been fighting Millsap's battles all of his life.

She was the older sister who lived as his mother. This was all ironic for me, for Millsap clearly loved his sister but was accused of killing two women. As a child, his sister loved him as a brother and a son.

When I first encountered Millsap, he figured not to be the thankless nigga I thought he was. He drew me a pencil drawing of Yogi Bear and gave it to me on one of my many visits. Millsap claimed that he didn't know why he was still being held and charged with murder since he had turned himself in to the police and all. Millsap claimed the death of his girlfriend was an accident. Him dragging her over 50 feet to the sewer and dropping her in head first was done because he was just scared, everybody should understand that.

Millsap swore to me that he had nothing to do with the death of the fat white woman found in his apartment two years before. He claimed that she owed money to some drug dealers. When she failed to pay, the drug dealers came inside his apartment and beat her to death. Millsap said that the drug dealers beat the white woman into a heart attack. I guess that could explain the black and blue bruises all over her body. The big bruise on her hip was when she fell over in her wheelchair and her weight against the arm of the wheelchair left quite a bruise. Ms. Ruby told me that Millsap loved that fat white woman. He'd push her around everywhere. Just as proud to have a white woman as any man.

Later, I found out different about what really happened to the white woman. But for now, it's all hearsay so I won't dare repeat it. Anyway, you know how niggas talk.

In my case, Millsap was accused of killing Lydia White. They had dated just over a year when Millsap paid her to perform a trick. They met near the West End over near the Atlanta University Center and fucked outside near some railroad tracks.

Both Millsap and Lydia hit it off and decided to date each other. I mean they would not be the first couple that stayed together because the sex was good or just out of convenience. Moreover, they were both crackhead drunks and homeless. So they would stay from cat hole to cat hole near and around the Atlanta University Center/ West End area of town.

I didn't know much more about Lydia. I didn't know who turned her out on drugs or how long she had been a trick. Her only adult son Doug told me he would find her on the street from time to time and give her money. As he got older, he would just bring her food, for he knew she would rather buy drugs than eat. Doug finally told me that he had enough horrible memories about his mother than to know that Millsap killed her and threw her head first in a sewer.

This whole conversation with Doug gave me pause. I couldn't help but internalize what Doug was telling me. I couldn't even imagine or dare to think of my mother as a trick, having to find her on the street to give her food. I'd like to think that I would have found her and brought her home.

I wondered if Doug even knew his father. Why was Doug gay? Was he born that way? Had one of his mother's tricks molested him? Or was it an uncle or cousin who molested him when he was too young to fend for himself? Did the molestation occur on one of those days when his momma was too high to give a damn? What was Doug's story?

Given all that Doug had gone through, he was a working man who appeared to be drug free, paid his taxes, and was living an otherwise normal life. Doug told me that he would learn to forgive Millsap, but he'd never forget the pain Millsap caused him. As Doug shared his story with me, his disposition was calm. However, his pain was exact and sharp. It moved me.

Millsap told me he had worked at the labor pool the day before and had made a little money. On the day of the murder, before he had left to return to the labor pool, he and Lydia ate breakfast at McDonald's. There, he gave Lydia five dollars to hold her until he got off later that evening. After work that day, Millsap said he went and cashed a $40 check from that day's work at the liquor store in the West End. He bought a half pint of gin and some food.

Millsap returned to the cat hole where he and Lydia and another couple stayed the night before. However, Lydia wasn't there. Millsap drank some of the gin before he started looking for Lydia. When he found Lydia, she was up near the same railroad tracks off of Martin Luther King Boulevard surrounded by a bunch of men. This is where he had had his first date with her.

As he got closer to the tracks, Millsap got shitty when he saw Lydia on her knees sucking this dude's dick. Millsap said that when he saw Lydia, she didn't have on any clothes or drawers. She was just wearing a shirt that covered just the top of her ass.

Millsap walked up on Lydia and the dude and confronted them. He asked the dude, "What the hell do you think you're doing?" The dude replied, "What does it look like? I gave her a half rock to suck my dick, so she's sucking my dick." Millsap told the dude that that was his woman. The dude then told Millsap, "Fuck both of ya'll" and took his half rock back. Lydia hadn't finished sucking his dick. An angry Lydia then told Millsap to go to hell.

As Millsap began to walk away, Millsap called Lydia a dirty BITCH. Anyone familiar with black women knows that no matter what a black woman's station or economic status is in life, you cannot call her a BITCH. I mean, you can do it but you just can't call her a BITCH and get away with it. It doesn't matter if she is a president of a company or a street walking crackhead ho. If you call her a BITCH, you got to fight. Lydia was no exception.

After Millsap called her a BITCH, Lydia got shitty and threw a brick at Millsap's head. Millsap ducked, picked up the same brick and threw it back at Lydia's head. Millsap told police that Lydia didn't duck. The brick struck her in the right temple.

Millsap said that after he hit Lydia with the brick, he got so drunk and high that he passed out. When he came to, everyone was gone. And, as far as he could tell, Lydia wasn't breathing. Lydia was dead.

Millsap said that another homeless dude told him that he couldn't leave her there. So, they drug all 240 pounds of Lydia 50 feet to the nearest sewer. It took both men, with their drunken asses, a while to lift the metal top off of the sewer. After they removed the top, they dropped Lydia into the sewer head first.

Lydia stayed in the sewer for about 10 days before the sewer department responded. They had received several calls of raw sewage backing into residences and the streets. The sewer man found Lydia, feet barely visible, protruding from the sewer in six feet of raw sewage. Thereafter, police and fire rescue were called to investigate the scene. The fire department had created a harness much like when you see an animal rescue. They placed the harness over the sewer and affixed straps to Lydia's ankles. They then pulled her rotten, rat-eaten decomposed body from the sewer.

While the extraction was in progress, Millsap, in his drunken crack-induced state happened upon the scene and told police he put the body in the sewer. Millsap was so fucked up and high, police told Millsap to beat it before they arrest him for disorderly conduct.

Millsap left the scene before turning himself in three weeks later. There were no suspects at the time Millsap turned himself in for the murder of Lydia White. The murder trial lasted for four days. Millsap was found not guilty of murder and felony murder. However, he was found guilty of voluntary manslaughter.

The District Attorney has decided not to pursue the murder of the fat white woman. Ms. Ruby was happy with the result of the trial. She didn't want her son/brother to spend the rest of his life in prison. Ms. Ruby died three weeks after the trial July 18, 2005.

Sentence: 15 years in prison.

PEPPER

A Love Story

Prince pounded on the door with the bottom of his fist — the police knock. Pepper knew her time was here and she had prepared for it. As Pooh opened the door, Prince saw the 9 mm pointed at the floor and then right at him. He and Pooh began to fight and struggle over the gun. The gun discharged and grazed Pooh in the hand. As he screamed out, Pepper slipped up behind Prince and shot him in the back with a .357 magnum. The force of the impact knocked Prince into the wall. He then fell to the floor on his back. Now crying like the bitch he was, Pooh stood over Prince and shot him in the stomach. Prince began to moan and cough up blood. Seemingly, Prince's injuries had taken all of the fight out of him.

After hearing the commotion, Ferdinand came out of Pepper's bedroom. Pepper started cursing and smacked the shit out of him because he didn't help with the ambush. Ferdinand just stood there dumbfounded like a lost child. All the while, Pooh was screaming like an old bitch. Eventually, he ran out of Pepper's house on the way to Grady Hospital.

Pepper then instructed Ferdinand to help her put Prince in the trap. As Ferdinand and Pepper grabbed Prince's shirt at the shoulders, they dragged him to the trap in Pepper's bedroom. The trap was a three-foot by three-foot cut in Pepper's bedroom floor that opened to the crawl space underneath the house. This is where Pepper would stash her drugs before she could package them. When they dropped Prince into the trap, Prince was still alive. He lasted about 30 minutes before he died. It takes about that long or less before your lungs fill up with blood and you suffocate.

Earlier that morning, the General had received a call from Prince. Prince told him to meet him at Pepper's house. Prince told the General that he had caught Pepper stealing money and drugs. Prince also told the General that Pepper had started her own crew. The General knew that he was to meet Prince at Pepper's house to kill her.

When the General pulled into Pepper's dirt makeshift driveway, he noticed Prince's van but Prince was not inside. Prince was to have waited for the General before confronting Pepper. As the General attempted to knock on Pepper's door, she opened the door. Before the General could say anything, Pepper told him that Prince and Pooh had taken her car to the corner store. The General knew that Pepper was lying, but he didn't see Prince or Pooh in the house. He figured to see at least one of them.

The General then left Pepper looking for Prince. He drove around the neighborhood because he didn't really know his way around. See, Prince, Pepper, and the General were part of a Jamaican Posse from the New York-Connecticut area. Prince was in charge. Pepper was to sell and the General was to do whatever Prince asked of him. When it came to Prince, Pepper, and the General, were like his jealous kids. They wanted both his time and attention. The General finally found the corner store. However, as he walked around the store he could not find Prince or Pooh. The General then asked a few crackheads if they had seen Pooh before returning to Pepper's.

Upon pulling into Pepper's driveway, Prince's van was gone. After the General had left for the store, Pepper had Ferdinand hide Prince's van. Ferdinand had driven the van to Duluth, Ga., about 40 minutes north from Pepper's house. Pepper told the General that Prince had left and to meet him in Cobb County. Cobb County is about 30 minutes west, in the opposite direction of Duluth. The General knew Pepper was lying, but he had no proof. Prince would not answer his cell phone and the General didn't want to smoke this bitch without confirming it with Prince. So the General just stayed parked in Pepper's yard for about an hour. He spent his time blowing up Prince's cell phone and debating on whether to kill this bitch. Eventually, the General left for Cobb.

After the General made it to Cobb, a few hours had passed and still no word from Prince. The General called Prince's lovers, the old and the new. They had not heard from Prince all day. Prince had even failed to pick up his new girlfriend from school, the Fashion Institute of Atlanta. Frustrated and confused, the General called Connecticut and New York. By nightfall, the Posse was on their way to Atlanta by car.

Prince had broken protocol. Prince knew he was to have waited on the General before confronting Pepper. Prince knew that after it was learned that Pepper was stealing, no confession was needed from Pepper. The folks back East had decided Pepper's fate. The General was to kill her and Prince was to replace her with another bitch, who would be sent down in a few days, no exceptions.

However, everybody had underestimated Pepper. Knowing the game as she did, Pepper got Prince before he could get her. To be slick and lose focus is one thing. To be slick and know when you've fucked up is another. They say an ounce of paranoia will keep you on your toes. Pepper knew that she had fucked up and she was one nasty, paranoid bitch.

Pepper was a 30-something Jamaican woman from the bush. She was dirt poor most of her life. Having an indoor toilet was a life change for her. Pepper had moved from the bowels of Jamaica to New York City as a young woman. Being schooled in the brutal drug game in Jamaica and New York, Pepper was not easily afraid of anything or anyone. Prince and Pepper had met in New York. They were a part of the same Jamaican Posse. When the posse decided to move to Atlanta, Prince was picked as the chosen one. Pepper was angered by this decision, because she was older than Prince and believed that she was more schooled in the game than he. By the time they made it to Atlanta, the animosity between the two was alive and well.

Prince lived in the upscale communities of Buckhead and Midtown. Pepper lived in the bowels of Atlanta. I remember when I was investigating the case, I went over to Pepper's place to interview a witness. The stench was so bad that I thought that I smelled dead bodies. I mean the smell was so bad that I couldn't get out of my truck without throwing up. So I interviewed the witnesses with my truck window substantially rolled up. Not knowing Pepper, I thought this was the type of area where Pepper felt more comfortable. Moreover, this was the type of crack-infested area that Pepper knew she could control.

The Posse would arrange the delivery and transportation of the drugs from the Connecticut-New York area to Prince here in Atlanta. Sometimes, Prince had to arrange for the transportation of the drugs himself. When this occurred, however, Prince would only use women to act as couriers. These women typically worked as strippers or at bars looking for a fast dollar. Prince insisted that none of the girls were users. Jamaicans, however, believed that smoking weed didn't count as being a crackhead. These couriers would take rental cars up and down Interstate 95 and cross over into Atlanta.

Prince would use another female to do an accounting of what was received. A call would then be placed to the East Coast to confirm delivery. Another female courier would take the drugs over to Pepper. Prince would tail the courier at a distance. The General would follow Prince in another car or just meet him at Pepper's house. In the event that Prince was stopped, no guns or drugs would be found on him. Driving that Mazda MPV van never attracted any attention and allowed Prince to creep. Then, Prince and Pepper would confirm with Connecticut and New York the quantity of what was given to her.

It has been known for years that Jamaican Posses didn't play. They are known to be as ruthless as the Asian gangs. For both gangs, death is merely a by-product of what one receives for coming up short and skimming money.

Just as Prince would use all women as couriers, Pepper would use all men. Pooh was her doorman. He was known to answer her door with his 9 mm in his hand. Pooh would become angry because Pepper would put him out of the house when Prince was present. For this, Pooh hated Prince and Prince had no respect for Pooh working for a bitch. Pooh sported a Barry White type of processed perm in his hair. He was about 6 feet tall and slender. He dressed like a ghetto thug walking around with his shirt opened and his dingy wife beater tee shirt underneath. There was nothing remarkable about the pants he would wear, only that he would keep his gun in his waistband.

Pooh had a newborn baby that was at most weeks old, but this did nothing to stop him from selling drugs out of the house. Pooh and his teenage girlfriend, the mother of his child, all lived with her elderly grandfather. Granddad could do nothing to control Pooh and his activities at his house, even if he wanted to. Granddad knew that keeping Pooh around was the only way to keep his granddaughter around, and he needed her help. Pooh tried to be a bully, but he was a wannabe thug who had no self-discretion. As I reflect back on Pooh, there was nothing cool about him. To the contrary, Prince dressed like a college boy, almost preppy, clean-shaven and very low-key.

Pepper either had severe acne or just plain bad skin. She was frumpy and very seldom combed her hair or used deodorant. Pepper's yellow teeth could give one the impression that Pepper brushed her teeth with butter. The hair underneath her armpits was short and nappy and to me, she gave pussy a bad name. She just appeared not to be concerned at all about hygiene even though she had a man — my client, Ferdinand. Pepper was also fucking one of her crackhead customers, Henry Mack.

Ferdinand was a 30-something year-old dude from the Bahamas. He had these bucked teeth and a huge overbite. I could see calmness in his smile. This made him either a cold-blooded killer or just a nice guy. He had a dark complexion with these dirty shoulder length dreads. Standing about 5'8," Ferdinand was a small man with slumped shoulders. He was a step away from being illiterate. This may have accounted for his low self-esteem. Initially, we had problems communicating, but I understood one thing that he conveyed to me and that was "mekillnooneman," "medidn'tkillthatboyman." Just like most of my clients, Ferdinand said that he was innocent.

Pepper kept a house full of crackheads around her like Tom and Betty O'Malley, Pepper's white neighbors thought they were black. Tom was a crackhead and Betty would just hang around to meet black guys. There was Billy Davis, the married smelly white male prostitute. Billy was also a crackhead. I think Billy had gotten turned out in prison. If not that, Billy was just a gay man who was married, which is very common in Atlanta. Billy had walked up to Pepper's door right after Prince. He heard the gunshots and he saw Pooh's bleeding hand before Pooh told him to get the hell on.

Henry Mack was a black dude in his late thirties. He was Pepper's other lover. Mack was just a crackhead who worked over at the University in the kitchen. Mack, however, was true to the game; he'd do or fuck anything for a hit of crack. That's the only way I could see him fucking Pepper.

Pepper convinced Tom to go dig a grave for her in one of the vacant lots up the street in exchange for crack cocaine. Tom went about the neighborhood looking for a shovel. He ran across Mr. Martin, an old retired railroad man. Tom asked Mr. Martin to borrow his shovel. He told Tommy that he could, but he needed to return it when he was through. Tommy gave Mr. Martin some bullshit reason why he needed the shovel but Mr. Martin didn't press the issue.

Tommy found a spot in one of the vacant lots and began digging a grave. After a few hours, Tommy returned to Pepper and told her he was done. Pepper sent Mack to the site to make sure it was deep enough. Mack reported to Pepper that the grave was too shallow. Tommy went back to the site and continued digging. Ferdinand and Mack helped dig this time. Thereafter, Mack told Pepper that it was cool.

Under the cover of night, Pepper instructed the three to remove Prince from the crawl space and bury him. By this time, Pooh had made it home from Grady. They all were talking about what happened earlier, when they began to move Prince. Half high and weak, they had trouble removing Prince from the crawl space. I guess dead weight in its literal since was heavier than they thought. Once they got Prince out of the crawl space, they knew that they had to find away to carry him to the gravesite up the street.

Pepper had an old grocery cart in the yard and Mack suggested that they use it. So Mack, Tommy, and Ferdinand put Prince's ass in the grocery cart the best they could and rolled him to the gravesite. The gravesite was at least 50 yards from Pepper's house. What a sight – a dread, a white boy, and a crackhead pushing a body down the street in a grocery cart.

Finding it difficult to push the cart over the vacant lot, they turned the cart over and drug Prince to the grave. After they reached the site, they just dropped Prince in to the grave. Tommy started covering the grave up first a shovel at a time, but he demanded that everyone help out in case someone decided to tell. Plus, it was too much work for Tommy to do himself. Pepper had instructed them to leave all of Prince's shit on his person and they did. His wallet, watch, and shoes were all with Prince when he was buried. The three of them got high off of weed and crack as they buried Prince. It took them over an hour to cover up Prince's body. Prince remained buried for two years.

The next day however, the posse was in town looking for Pepper and they found her at home. The posse wanted to know where Prince was. Even though no one at the trial ever identified the people that consisted of the posse – and there were many – we referred to them as one. Pepper swore to them that she didn't know where Prince was. The posse then kidnapped her and Ferdinand and drove them around town until they found a spot. There, they stripped them down to their underwear and commenced to whip their asses, especially Pepper's.

The General and Mia were with the posse when they got to Atlanta. Mia was Prince's old girlfriend. Ah, Mia. Mia was about 6 feet tall without heels and about 6'2 or 6'3" with her shoes on. She had LPH (long pretty hair) that reached her middle back. Her back was long and slender and fell right into her apple bottom butt. With her Caramel brown complexion, Mia was a stallion.

Sadly, Mia was a dope girl and that's all she dated. Mia wanted the high life and the dope boys gave that to her. Mia was the mother of twins that Prince had taken care of for a long time, even though Prince wasn't their father. Prince was good to Mia while it lasted but he was evolving. Prince had started to turn the corner. He had purchased a restaurant in a neighboring county. He was paying for the new girl to go to college. Still, Prince took care of Mia and the twins and she appreciated it. Mia still loved Prince in spite of the fact that she knew Prince was changing and she did not fit in to those plans. Mia knew that she wasn't the college type and the new girlfriend represented the direction Prince's life was headed in. As to not make a scene and to help Mia out, Prince kept Mia on the payroll. Mia did move to Atlanta for him.

Mia begged the posse to kill Pepper or to let her do it. Instead, Mia was only allowed to smack or punch a naked restrained Pepper around. Eventually, Pepper reminded the posse of all of the money they stand to lose with her and Prince out of the picture. Police estimated that Pepper and Prince were operating a million dollar drug business.

Pepper told the posse that she had taken the beating and she still didn't know where Prince was. Maybe it was Prince who skipped on them and not her; they did find her at home. If she had done something to Prince, don't you think she would have fled as opposed to waiting on them to come kill her? Pepper convinced them that they were wasting time and money. Since in the dope game, it's all about the money, they let Pepper go. The subject of her stealing never came up again.

Two years later, Mr. Martin's dog came home with a bloody shoe. Mr. Martin followed the dog to the area where the dog found the shoe. There, he found the shovel he let Tommy use and never returned. Mr. Martin then saw Prince's partially unearthed body. Prince had been found. Mr. Martin called police.

Police came and excavated Prince's body from the grave. Prince's watch was still affixed to what was his arm. After seeing the watch, the police knew that Prince's murder did not involve a robbery.

Things started to unravel when the neighbors started talking about the dead body being found in the lot. Billy, the male prostitute, had gotten arrested on the strip trying to sell some ass. Remember, he actually saw Prince at Pepper's door and he saw Pooh bleeding right after the shooting. He had gone to Pepper's place to buy some crack when the shit was going down. Seemingly, he was the last person to see Prince alive. In working a deal for himself, he told police about the shooting he saw at Pepper's place. "You know, the boy y'all found in the vacant lot, I think I know who killed him," Billy said.

In speaking with police, Billy told on Tommy, Tommy told on Pepper, Pepper told on Ferdinand and Pooh, but not on Henry Mack, her other man. Mr. Martin told police about his shovel found at Prince's gravesite he'd allowed Tommy to use. Police rounded up this crew and everybody started telling on each other. Ferdinand told police about Mack, but tried to protect Pepper. Pepper accused Ferdinand and Pooh, her doorman of the murder. Mack's name never came out of Pepper's mouth.

The district attorney indicted Tommy and his sister, Sherry. I guess Sherry was indicted because she hung out with Pepper. Pepper, Ferdinand, Mack, and Pooh were also indicted. Eventually, the district attorney dismissed its case against Sherry. However, Tommy and Mack got a slap on the wrist for burying Prince. Pepper pled guilty to voluntary manslaughter and was sentenced to 12 years in exchange for her testimony at trial.

When the trial started, it was Ferdinand and Pooh at the table. I don't recall who represented Pooh. I just remember Pooh with his processed hair and scraggly beard. The state put up all of these co-defendants as witnesses and the police officers. Mia admitted on the stand how she gave Pepper a beat down and that she was, in fact, a dope girl. I accused Pooh of killing Prince out of jealousy and instructions from Pepper. I also accused Pooh of wanting to be Prince.

Of course, Pooh denied everything and blamed Ferdinand and Pepper for Prince's murder. But he had nothing to say when I accused him of selling his drugs around his newborn baby. Pepper admitted that she paid Pooh in drugs, not money.

I questioned Prince's mother about who Prince was, a common drug dealer. To my surprise, the General admitted that he was Prince's enforcer. The District Attorney had brought the General in from a federal prison to testify. He had been convicted on unrelated charges or he had violated his federal probation. I mean, I was as nasty to Pooh as I was to Prince's mother. There were over thirty witnesses that testified and I was ready for all of them except one.

The court was in recess and the state had one witness left. I had left the courtroom for water when I encountered this lady in a brown pin-striped suit in the hallway. Her hair was slicked down like Josephine Baker. I mean, she was dressed and her style was from another time. She had this smooth brown complexion and elegant looking hands. She wanted to make eye contact with me just as much as I wanted to with her. So we looked in each other's direction. When I looked at her, I said hello with a smile. She looked at me up and down and rolled her eyes. Her neck went from side to side like she was from India or something.

I just kept walking and eventually I made it to the restroom, I mean water fountain. The Assistant District Attorney was a long time friend and law school buddy I had met in Houston, Texas over 10 years ago. I asked him about the lady in the brown suit, he told me that she was Prince's younger sister. We agreed that she was cute and fine as hell.

As my buddy questioned her, she testified that she was a Fordham Graduate and had her master's degree in education. She taught third grade in New York City. I thought to myself that Prince paid for her education. Even if he didn't, from everything that I heard about Prince, he would have.

As she testified, I reflected on how I actually respected Prince. He was not the typical drug dealer who drove the expensive luxury car or wore flashy clothes. Prince didn't wear loud expensive jewelry. He operated in the shadows. He drove a minivan. His new girlfriend was a college girl. Prince helped his mother and sister out financially. He was a good father to his only son. I just didn't like what Prince did for a living. He knowingly sold poison to people — crack.

It was now my turn to question Prince's sister. I stood up at my table and looked her in the eyes. I told the Judge, no questions. Prince's sister was disappointed. She wanted to take me. She wanted to deal with me as I had dealt with her mother and Mia. She wanted to get some closure through confrontation with me, but I wouldn't give it to her. It wasn't about her anyway; it's about my client.

As the jury began to deliberate, Pooh pled guilty to 12 years in prison for voluntary manslaughter. He got the same deal as Pepper. The jury found Ferdinand not guilty of murder, but could not decide on the rest. Retrial, we have to do this shit all over again.

It would be months before we'd start the process again. However, weeks after the trial, I got a call from the District Attorney's Office. It was an elderly receptionist that was a good friend of mine. She told me that there was someone trying to get in touch with me. But she found it odd, so she called me to see if it was okay to give the caller my number. I told her it was fine.

Within minutes, I got a call from New York City. It was Prince's sister Amanda, the schoolteacher. I, of course, wanted to know why she was calling. She told me that the call was social and that she didn't want to talk about the case. I told her that I didn't feel comfortable talking with her, since the case was still pending. She ignored my concerns and we talked all night. It seems we talked by phone until she ended up on my doorstep here in Atlanta.

She stayed here three days with a cousin. We started making plans for her to relocate to Atlanta. However, we were both in relationships. She was dating a professional football player for the Philadelphia Eagles, and I was dating a single mom from Washington D.C. who I dearly cared for. Within minutes, I started tripping, thinking this was nothing but a setup. I thought that she was trying to play me to have me disqualified from representing Ferdinand. But as she kissed and held me, I knew it was only about us.

I told her that I was afraid of her because Mia had come onto me as well. Unlike her, Mia lived here in Atlanta. She asked me if I wanted her or Mia, and I told her I wanted her and we never spoke of Mia again.

When the second trial started, it was apparent to me that her mother did not know the extent of our friendship. After a day in court, her mother caught me in Amanda's hotel room. She told Amanda to be careful with me. I didn't tell her that Amanda called me, but the look on Amanda's face was one that said I was the one for her. I felt the same way. Amanda had made her mind up about me and not even her own Momma or dead brother could stop her.

Ferdinand's second trial lasted as long as the first one — two weeks. He was convicted of voluntary manslaughter.

Amanda never relocated to Atlanta. She had gotten a promotion within the school district she wanted. She started her own business and things were going well for her in New York. She told me she met a good guy who adores her. They have been together over five years now and they have taken a pledge of celibacy. She and I still talk. On one occasion, I told her that I was coming to New York to visit. She told me that she was not ready to see me yet. Funny, how she assumed that I was coming to see her. Like me, she knows that anytime, anyplace, we could just be.

Ferdinand was sentenced to 12 years in prison. His case was reversed on appeal. Ferdinand was paroled in 2004. I never told Ferdinand about Amanda.

THE CIVILITY OF PURPOSE

When I got out of my car, I heard a voice call my name. It was a sweet voice, genuine and sincere. "Hello, Mr. Johnson," she called to me again. When I saw who it was that was speaking to me, my world stopped. I was lost for words and she could tell. It was Ms. Helen. Lost in my awkwardness, she made it clear that it was cool-and that she was cool. See, whatever I was tripping about or whatever I was concerned about didn't matter now, today. It didn't matter in the moment that we encountered each other. There was something else going on. There was no need to rehash how we met or why. There was something new in the present that she had on her mind; that something was in the moment.

I tried to say I was sorry but she interrupted me. She didn't want to hear it. She said, "I know it's just a job for you." I was taken back by her resolve. The peace in her heart caused me to pause. She was being civil to me. Recognizing her civility, I was humbled by her.

If the shoe were on the other foot, I don't know if I could have been as civil and kind to her. Sometimes it's harder for me to be friendly than it is for me to be frank because I'm petty. I know that

I take things personally. I hold on to shit for a long time, even down to the lack of a return phone call. But she was civil to me.

Civility, I don't know if it's a Southern thing but it is a mannerism that is practiced more often in the South than anywhere I've been. I didn't find much of it in Chicago nor did I find much of it outside of my neighborhood growing up in Indianapolis. Civility causes one to reciprocate the gestures and tone of politeness out of mutual respect. Comport one's conduct to act with courtesy and self-awareness with a stranger or friend about a subject. It gives the conversation a quiet dignity that prevents it from digressing to one of rudeness or condescension.

Civility is so rare nowadays that when one sees it, one becomes guarded and uncomfortable. When the act of civility expresses itself, some become suspicious and perceive it as an act of ill-will. I think a generation or two has been lost without civility. Sadly, they've never learned that civility is the foundation for a moral code.

My parents were from Mississippi, they taught the seven of us manners and how to act civilized, as they would put it. Being the youngest, I was taught by my older siblings as they taught their children who were my age and older. The education in manners was not optional. To show a lack of home training was considered an embarrassment to the family. This offense was punishable by a beating with a broom, mop or an extension cord. We prayed for punishment by belt.

I ran into Ms. Helen at a Kinko's copying center. As I tell this story, I don't recall why I was there. I probably had to copy a file for a case. However, she was there to make copies of her son's obituary. He was murdered in Southeast Atlanta a few days ago. I thought to myself, God, don't you have someone who will do that for you? My answer was in seeing her there alone. Her son was only a teenager or possibly in his early twenties.

She told me that she was trying to raise money to cover the funeral expenses. When she asked me for money, I knew God was reeling me in again. I know that I get caught up representing those that kill people. I don't know why I do, but it's what I do. I'm fascinated with those who murder. I'm fascinated with their motivation of how they come to murder or did murder come to them; self-defense. I handle these situations as I would want someone to handle mine, if I killed.

Ms. Helen told me that she was really having trouble coming up with the funds to bury her son and that she would accept a contribution from me. I couldn't believe that she was talking to me but she was. It was such a beautiful day. It was early Saturday morning and the Georgia sun was out but it wasn't humid. I could breathe. The grass was wet from last night's rain. It was a beautiful day for a funeral.

She was rushed because she had to be at the church with the obituaries for the 1 o'clock service. When we spoke, she apologized for not being able to talk longer. Again, she told me that she understood that I was just doing my job and she didn't take anything personally.

People walked around us as we talked in the copying center like we were old friends. They didn't know that a few months before, I had represented Cory, the kid who was convicted of killing Ms. Helen's grandbaby. Ms. Helen had to find the strength to bury her grandbaby that was barely a year old. Today, Ms. Helen now had to bury her teenage son, the baby's father, in the same year.

The crushing pain that some people endure is hard for me to imagine. It's beyond my comprehension how they come to survive it. They somehow keep going through their faith, hope, or belief that change is going to come in spite of the pain. For them, things will somehow get better. In her pain, she was civil to me, even cordial. Perhaps that's just what adults do, carry their pain and disappointments around and still are able to smile. She had character.

Cory was only 18 years old and an only child. His mother was extremely obese. I don't know if Cory even knew his dad. His mother, however, spoiled him to death. Like most kids, Cory was really loved by his mother and he knew it. However, Cory had become a spoiled, selfish, self-centered little prick. I know that many people spoil their children. I would spoil my own if I had some. I, like most, would want to teach them the difference between right and wrong. I would want to teach them how to share with the less fortunate, to have a sense of charity and God. I don't think that Cory ever got that from home. If he did, he had lost it somewhere.

With Cory's father being absent in his life, Cory learned how to be a man in the streets. I remember meeting his mother on occasions. She needed to take breaths between sentences. Her teeth would sandwich her tongue when she spoke. Then, there would be another deep breath and another thought. I thought her to be lazy and unmotivated to allow herself to get so obese. Then I thought of my own mother, who was bigger than she. Mother rose for work at about 4 a.m. every day of my life. Nine kids later (two died, one of sudden infant death syndrome and another at childbirth), she taught me to love my brothers and sisters and to mind my own business. She introduced me to God; she taught me how to be me.

Cory's mother worked at the local newspaper. I don't know what her job title was, but I would see her from time to time. My office was less than a half of block from hers. Maybe she worked just as hard as my mother did. Perhaps, I was too quick to judge her overcompensation of affection for Cory.

I don't know if this was the first time that Cory was getting steady pussy or not. Perhaps, it could have been just the newness of Cory thinking himself to be a dad. At any rate, Karen would tell Cory that the baby was his when she needed things. When she didn't need shit, she'd tell Cory that another fathered the baby. At 18 years old, Cory wanted to be a father. Like many misguided teens, fatherhood was his license to manhood. Because of his child, he now had a purpose for living. He had someone else to love unconditionally, like a son. This, seemingly, was another cruel joke God has played on me for all of my pussy chasing ways. I guess I should be thankful. One of my brother's blessings was five daughters for the same offense.

Cory was short, about 5'7," and still teenage skinny. He had broad shoulders and a slight mustache that accented his light brown complexion. His hair was cut short but he wasn't clean-shaven. He was by far one of my dumbest clients or just teenage stupid. It took time to understand what Cory was saying. He would even say his name in a way that made you ask for it again.

Karen was this tiny little thing. She was slightly darker than Cory. She sat at counsel's table with her feet dangling, barely touching the floor. She had a slight overbite and appeared to be a 12-year-old from her small stature. Apparent was her low self-esteem, as she sat there mousy with her slumped shoulders hiding her small breasts. I noticed how Karen was so absorbed in the fear and immaturity that comes with being 17 and on trial for the murder of your own baby.

As I looked around the courtroom for her absent mother, I had conflicting feelings for Karen that vacillated between empathy and disgust. I had my ideas on how Karen became what she was, a teenage mother. I could only hope that after this experience, she and Cory would become better people as I had wished for my own niece who is a teenage mom of two, and her brother who is a teenage father to a son. The more I delved into this case, the more reflections of my life stare at me. I can't ever cast the first stone or any stone for that matter.

On the day in question, like most teenagers, Cory and Karen could not afford a motel room. So they fucked in his car. I guess Karen, on this particular night, told Cory that it really wasn't his baby. They fucked all night; when they woke up the baby was dead. They claimed that they didn't know what happened to the baby. However, the medical examiner claimed that the baby had bruises old and new all over his body. Everyone knew that Karen was the baby's primary caretaker. So she had to be responsible for the old bruises. Moreover, you could tell she was the type to leave the baby with just anybody. Karen would even leave the baby with Cory or his Mother to go fuck the baby's father. I guess that was okay, it's her pussy. It just seemed foul to me when I heard about it. However, I've been accused of placing too much value on pussy anyway. That old 'who fucked whom' thing is really obsolete, if not cliché.

At trial, the detectives described how Karen would laugh as they interviewed her about the baby's death, no tears. But who am I to say how 17-year-olds grieve under the stress of being accused of murdering one's baby. I know that many people laugh when they are nervous. I'm just not one of them. And I don't laugh to be polite when the joke's not funny; particularly racial jokes because I know that I'm the brunt of the joke when I'm not around.

They told police that they fucked as teenagers do, all night. They couldn't remember if they had put the baby in the backseat and they were in the front seat or if they were in the backseat. However, they did recall the baby crying all night. When the baby cried, Karen would tend to it. Sadly, when they woke up the next morning, the baby was dead.

Cory said that when he saw that the baby wasn't breathing, he picked it up and ran to the neighboring apartment complex for help. In the end, Cory was just a crying adolescent who offered the baby to anyone who would help. But no one would touch the baby. The neighbors knew that the baby was dead. Cory franticly knocked on several doors of the apartment complex for help, but to no avail. The baby was still dead. Sadly, no one saw Karen crying as she just stood near Cory and the baby. Karen said nothing.

Her attorneys claimed that Karen didn't say anything because she was in shock. I didn't buy that reason simply because when faced with death, black folks will clown. There is no quiet dignity when black folks die. They scream and fall out on the floor only to be restrained and do it all over again.

At trial, like children, I blamed Karen and Karen's attorneys blamed Cory for the baby's death. It didn't matter though; the jury saw through our adversarial confusion and convicted both of them of voluntary manslaughter.

All of these thoughts were running through my mind as I engaged Ms. Helen in conversation. Before long, she was gone. I don't know if I gave her a contribution at the copying center because I usually don't carry cash on me. I'd like to think that I sent her something in the mail; I just don't know if I did. I wanted to and the fact that I can't remember troubles me. It would have been the only civil thing to do.

Karen's case was reversed on appeal. She is now out of prison.
Cory was paroled in 2008.

Chapter 3

Drugs

DINNER WILL BE SERVED AT THE CHURCH

Praised by his football coach, Anthony was carried to his final resting place by his teammates. Atlanta was hurt. She was mourning the death of another teenager. This time, one of her shining stars. Anthony was a true ghetto success story in the making. Unlike many kids from the ghetto, Anthony had promise. He was expected to be many things: a businessperson, a professional athlete, or anything he wanted to be. It was there for him. We've heard time and time again that somehow this kid was bigger, better and more special than the next. But in Anthony's case, it was true.

He was only 15 years old, 6'3" tall, and an honor student. Anthony was handsome and doted a pearly white smile. Anyone with a heart would have wanted Anthony to succeed in life. He was the son that every parent wanted as his own. He was that kid that all the other kids wanted as their friend.

Anthony was mature for his age because he had to be. He lived near the McDaniel Glenn Housing Projects in southeast Atlanta. For the most part, this was just like any other ghetto, lawless and violent. I'm not to saying that everyone in the projects are bad people. In fact, I think you have more people in the projects that work hard every day trying to improve their circumstances. Wall Street refers to them as the working poor. This class included Anthony and his mother, Vanessa.

Anthony, a product of a single-parent home, was our promise of things to come; the rare example that one could outrun the violence in one's environment. But here we are again. We've lost another one.

Other than Rudy being a product of the same environment, I can't say that it was anyone's fault that Anthony was killed. Somehow, an AK-47 assault rifle just made it into the hood. On this day like many others, police had no way of knowing that they needed to protect Anthony. Moreover, his mother had no way of knowing that renegade street violence would claim another victim, this time her son.

If Atlanta had known, she would have helped and protected Anthony the best she could. She would've saved his life for life's sake. He was worth saving.

The issue of teenagers killing other teenagers is puzzling to all. Parents are not supposed to outlive their kids — so we think — but when you live in a ghetto, the rules of society changes. For each ghetto is its own vacuum with its own rules. Anthony had to be mature and careful because he lived in a vacuum and he knew of such violence. Not that he was a violent person, it's just impossible to be exposed to violence everyday and not become aware of it.

Some people may become numb to the everyday violence in their neighborhood. Or as witnesses, they become more and more casual about the acts of violence that they've seen. Even as kids, you learn to live side-by-side with crackhead whores and dope boys. Just as the working folks, these folks are all part of the neighborhood make up. Such as the Arabs or Asians that run the hole-in the-wall store. After a while, even their children begin to imitate ghetto behavior. Before long, one of the many kids that see ghetto behavior will begin to imitate and identify with it as normal. To the contrary, at 15, Anthony had other plans for himself. He would not be identified by the color of the T-shirt he wore.

Seemingly, when a teen is killed, we question ourselves. We even question our religion. We ask ourselves rhetorical questions like, "Are we truly the products of our environment?" We know that some of us get out of the ghetto alive, but are permanently scarred by what we've experienced.

On the other hand, we know that some of us never get out. Thus, they never change their behavior or know the difference in how life could be with a simple change of environment. Usually, this group contains those that blame the white man for their poverty and helplessness in the community. They seek to blame others for their own lack of initiative to change.

Sadly, there are those like Anthony who never make it out. They never make it out not because of something they did or didn't do. They never make it out just because they lived there. They lived in a ghetto and they died there. With no logical explanation for their untimely death, society keeps moving on. It's not that she doesn't care; it's just that she has her own shit to carry. Thus, the death of a teen is accepted as just another victim of street violence.

Anthony's death is further evidence that the government's sociological experiments of housing projects for low-income people have failed. To me, it's funny how some of our brightest flowers can still grow in between the cracks in the sidewalk, and cacti are able to grow in the desert. Just like our teenage children, it doesn't matter that both the flower and the cactus are self-sustaining. Like the flower and cati, our children are still delicate. Just like our teenage children, each can be killed by the simplest and dumbest of inhumane acts.

Anthony's mother, Vanessa, worked in the same building as I and on the same floor. She had been a manager at some check cashing, short-term finance loan company. These companies would usually prey on the poor. They would extend a 300-dollar loan to you at 31 percent interest over a three-month period. They would even penalize you if you paid the loan off too early. The interest was on the whole $300, and not the balance of the loan as you pay it down. These companies are all around Atlanta and are nothing less than legalized loan sharks.

I had been in this particular building for about five years. Vanessa was there, I know for as long, in the office around the corner from me. The men's restroom and a water fountain separated our offices. As long as I had been there, Vanessa was very pleasant to everyone. She was always smiling, always speaking. She was the type of person you didn't mind having a superfluous conversation with on more than one occasion during the day.

I didn't know anything about her personal life nor did she know anything about mine. I didn't know if she was married or not or whether she had kids. I didn't know if she was actually from Atlanta since no one else is.

Vanessa sported a weave ponytail that fell to her middle back. The space between her teeth and her caramel brown complexion reminded me of my mother. She was either in her late thirties or early forties. She was just a pleasant person I would run into everyday for about five years of my life.

I had learned of her son's death from another lawyer that was my office neighbor. I think that several offices on the floor took up a collection for the funeral. I don't remember if I gave or not. I'm sure, however, if I were there I would have contributed something. At the time, I knew her son had been killed, but I didn't know any details of the murder.

I never personally approached Vanessa to give my condolences or anything. I think I may have even forgotten about her loss soon after the funeral. Not that I didn't care, it's just that Vanessa wasn't a part of my life for me to carry her pain for too long, if at all. I mean, I, just like everybody else, is saddened when a teen is gunned down in the streets. The fact that it was Vanessa's son caused me some pause. But, I guess at the time, Anthony was just another ghetto boy killed in a drive-by shooting.

Months later, I received a call from the courthouse. I don't know if it was from a judge or her assistant. They wanted to know if I would represent a teenager accused of killing another teenager. At the time, I said sure, I'd be glad to. Little did I know that the teenager in question was the young man that was accused of killing Anthony, Vanessa's son.

As with any case, I first start a file on the client. I then begin the process of collecting police reports and all to prepare a defense. For me, every defense starts out the same. Firstly, my client wasn't there and if he was there, he didn't do it and if he did do it, it was self-defense.

On a Saturday evening, Jason, a friend of Anthony's, had stopped by his apartment to show off the car he just purchased. There was nothing special about Jason's car other than it was Jason's first car and he wanted to show it to his friend. I think it was a blue, 4-door Buick Le Saber. Jason had bought the car days before from Maurice, a known drug dealer from People's Town, another weed seed community in Southeast Atlanta.

As drug dealers go, Maurice had many enemies. His enemies would range from battles over drug turf to beefs over the amount of drugs sold and monies paid. Police knew of Maurice. They considered him a small time player, a minor leaguer; a wannabe thug. I don't think the police took Maurice seriously.

Maurice would do business out of his car. He knew that the car was hot before he sold it to Jason. Maurice, however, never told Jason about the car or to be cool when riding through certain areas. One would think that Jason should have already known about the car. But just like any other teenager buying their first car, the whole buyer beware thing got lost.

My client, Rudy could not have been 18 years old himself. Semiliterate and teenage goofy, Rudy was of no help to me in preparing for his defense. This was not surprising to me since most of my clients will inevitably go with my version of how the crime occurred over their own. My version seems to always suggest that the client is innocent.

To me, my client's confession to this strange authoritative cop is always treated as suspicious. Secondly, if there were any eyewitnesses to the alleged crime, they were mistaken. Thus, it wasn't my client they saw, even if they knew him by name. It was simply someone who looked like him.

The scenario usually works like this:

Q: You did not give the police my client's name as the shooter did you? **A:** No, I didn't know your client's name.

Q: How do you know that it was my client you saw that night? **A:** I saw your client's face and his dreadlocks.

Q: Did you look my client in the face when you saw him? **A:** No, I saw the side of his face.

Q: Were his dreadlocks unique in any way? Once you saw the dreads, you knew it was my client? **A:** No.

Q: So when looking at the suspect from the side, his face looked like my client? **A:** Yes.

Q: So, that night, in this moving van, shots were fired and you saw someone who resembled my client? **A:** Yes.

Q: When the shots rang out, did you run away from the van or towards the van? **A:** Away from the van.

Q: Would that be at the time you saw the side of the suspect's face? **A:** Yes, I thought it was him.

Q: So, my client only looks like the person you saw?

A: Yes. He kind of looks like him but I don't know for sure. I was running myself. I was trying not to get shot.

I usually can glean from the police reports of how the crime actually occurred. This approach allows me to imagine the successful outcome of my case, notwithstanding how the client feels. Getting the client off on a lesser offense is cool, but it doesn't get my dick as hard as winning.

Not winning at all cost, but an occasional understatement isn't lying. Besides, people expect me to lie a little, especially if I'm representing them or a loved one. On the other hand, jurors just figure if the trial goes on long enough, they'll catch my client or me in a lie sooner or later. When that happens, the case is usually over. To the contrary, if we're able to sneak by, the jury may just deliberate like they're suppose to.

Anthony and Rudy didn't know each other and had never met. Rudy had gotten his ass beaten down by Maurice some days ago over drug turf. Rudy confronted Maurice about selling drugs on his turf when Maurice jumped out of his car and began whipping Rudy's ass in front of everybody. Rudy felt like he had been punked by Maurice and essentially, he had.

I don't know if Maurice thought the beef between he and Rudy was over or if he expected Rudy to seek revenge. But at any rate, Maurice didn't have Rudy in mind when he sold his car to Jason. Maurice never told Jason anything about Rudy. Maurice was into so much shit, I don't know if his run-in with Rudy was any more important to him as anything else he had done.

Unbeknownst to Rudy, Maurice had sold his car to Jason. Rudy, while riding around in his mother's car, saw what he had believed to be Maurice's car parked near Anthony's apartment. Rudy left the scene and returned home to get his AK- 47 assault rifle. Rudy then returned in a stolen church van to where he had seen Maurice's car.

Some days ago, Rudy's older brother had stolen the church van from the neighborhood church. When Rudy returned to the car, Jason and Anthony were just sitting in the car making plans. Much like any teenager, they were excited about the car and about having transportation to and from the parties. Jason had promised to let Anthony hold it from time to time after he got his driver's license. For them, the summer was looking better and better.

Jason's car was parked facing the north so that he was closer to the street. Anthony was sitting on the passenger's side, when the van's driver pulled up and fired. Jason had time to duck but he still got hit in the wrist. Anthony was struck in his side underneath his armpit. Anthony never had a chance, as the bullet ripped through his heart and lungs. Anthony died on the scene.

The neighbors ran to Vanessa's apartment and told her the news. They said she had an emotional breakdown right there on the street. She held on to Anthony as the neighbors tried to console her away. They said that Vanessa held onto Anthony as she coached and begged him to keep breathing. Like any mother, she didn't want to believe that her son was dead, but he was. When police arrived, they began to console Vanessa and she finally let Anthony go. Atlanta began to cry.

I've had experience with a parent losing a child. My sister Helen lost her baby when I was about 12 years old. I never knew what emotional pain was until that time. Even today, my niece's death is my benchmark for pain. Whatever happens to me either hurts as much or less than my niece's death. My mother's own death didn't compare.

My niece had been born prematurely and had fought for life for two years. It was my first experience with death. I remembered how my sister screamed, as if God himself didn't love her. My brother Randy fell on top of her, screaming just as loudly. I didn't know what to do, but as a child I looked to my mother. And, as a child, if my mother cried, I cried. It seemed like God gave my niece to us just long enough to have hoped that she would live. And then he took her away. Since that day, I've never felt pain like that.

Randy, however, died when I was 24 years old. My mother, upon learning of his death, asked God to take her instead. She said this as if she were chanting and praying at the same time. Then, I didn't understand why my mother would make such a prayer. There were six of us left and we loved her just as much as Randy. But she continued to pray for death before she resigned from living — her spiritual death.

It was clear to me that she had given up on life when she made that prayer to God. I guess she couldn't take seeing another one of her children leave this earth before her. After Randy died, my mother was never the same. The following year, she was diagnosed with Alzheimer's. Ten years later, she died her physical death.

Even though I was 34 years old when my mother died, I never had an adult conversation with her. Now Vanessa would never see her boy grow up or meet his wife. She too would never have an adult conversation with her son or hold his children, her grandbabies. Seemingly, Rudy had taken everything that Vanessa had. Anthony was an only child.

The police had easily linked the stolen church van to Rudy's brother. It took all of 10 minutes before he gave Rudy's name to the police claiming that it was Rudy who had the van during the time of the shooting. Some people believe that he was the driver of the van and Rudy was the shooter. I mean how does one fire an AK-47 and drive a church van at the same time? But as it was, Rudy was the only person charged with Anthony's murder and I was his lawyer.

Rudy was about 5'10" and weighed about 150 pounds. He wore these 10-inch long dreadlocks that didn't compliment his appearance. I'm sure his dreadlocks were just an element of style for him. I could glean from just looking at him that he didn't know that dreads were part of a culture that practiced a wholesome lifestyle or way of life. Rudy also had these yellow-stained bucked teeth that made it difficult for me to understand him. He was a high school dropout and semi-literate.

Rudy and his three brothers were all living with their mother. She, a self-proclaimed church lady, figured to be just like the rest of us. At trial, it came out that she had lied to police on Rudy's behalf. Little did she know that Rudy's brother told police details about what had occurred before they interviewed her. This didn't surprise me. Most parents would lie for their child. I never had a parent that wouldn't help provide an alibi for their child, if I needed one.

I never met Rudy's mother in person. I thought this to be odd since Rudy was but a baby himself. Usually I become the parental figure for my young clients, but Rudy was on his own. Even before

I knew that he killed Vanessa's son, I didn't have much of a connection with Rudy.

On the morning of trial, I would usually try to be the first person in the courtroom. Much like a dog, I like to be the first one to piss on what I claim as my territory. As I entered into the courtroom and I saw Vanessa sitting in there with an elderly lady. I assumed that she was there as a court spectator. I'm like Vanessa, fancy meeting you here. What brings you to the ghetto? For the first time, Vanessa told me that I represent the young man that killed her only child. Damn.

I could have tried to get off the case, but I didn't know Vanessa that well. The loss of her son and my representation of his killer were more coincidental and awkward than personal. If I had only worked on a different floor, I'd take the chance encounter with Vanessa at the elevator. But, as it turns out, Vanessa is someone that I saw almost every day for the past five years.

On all those occasions, she and I would ride up the elevator together, and I would wonder how long she'd known that I represented her son's killer. She never let on that she knew. She was just as polite and congenial as always. The way of which she composed and handled herself was always ladylike. Truly, she had her reasons for not bringing it up. But I just didn't know what they were.

In the courtroom, I wondered if she thought my reaction was insincere. I really wanted to impress upon her that I had just found out that Anthony was her son. Even still, she looked me straight in the eyes and told me that it was okay. At that point, I knew then that Vanessa was better than me.

I have always been one to choose sides and I wanted everyone to know whose team I was on. It would be hypocritical of me to say otherwise. Law has always been a part of the judgment business. More often than not, it's a case of who can judge thy neighbor accurately that separates good lawyers from the mediocre.

The trial lasted for about four or five days. Jason testified about seeing the van pull up and the gunfire. He identified Rudy as the shooter. The police officers testified about how the church van led them to Rudy's brother, which led them to Rudy. Based on that evidence, Rudy was convicted of Anthony's murder.

At the funeral, I heard they were all at the church — Anthony's teammates, friends, neighbors, ministers, and dignitaries. At the funeral, the Mayor showed up and it wasn't even an election year.

So they all assembled at the church. I heard they talked about teen violence and how easily guns made it into the ghetto. Basically, they talked about the same old shit they talk about at every tragedy. A few other ministers got up and said some words to the congregation. Some even tried to use Anthony's death to preach their coming out sermon.

However, after the mayor spoke and the ministers said their final words, the tears slowed. Again, the ministers preached about optimism. I heard that the officiating minister then stood up from of his throne that was placed center mass in the pulpit and cleared his throat. He wiped his brow as he glanced out over the congregation and announced what everybody had been waiting for, simply that after they returned from the gravesite, dinner would be served at the church. Anthony's football team had dedicated their season in his honor. They lost every game.

Sentence: Life in prison plus 20 years.

GET OFF THE PORCH

Diddy was only 17 when he was accused of murder. Witnesses claimed that a white man drove up to the drug trap in Fourth Ward looking to buy a hit or two of crack cocaine when all the young men trapping rushed his car. Clearly, he couldn't buy everything that was offered to him. So he had to make a choice. When he chose another's drugs over Diddy's, they claimed that Diddy shot and killed him.

The dope boys refer to the location or place where they sell their drugs as a trap in a figurative sense. In most cases, there's only one way in and out of the trap. However, some traps come equipped with escape routes in case of police raids, and all traps have a place where the drugs are kept before they are sold. The drug user is considered the prey and the dealer is the predator. The prey is simply someone trapped in his or her addiction. The predator is trapped because the drug money comes easily and in abundance. Besides, as a square, the dealer doesn't know what else he can do to make as much money as he does selling drugs.

Albeit fear and old age are the two things that will change the dope boys' perspective on a life of trapping, in most cases, they wait too late to make a difference in their life. The dope boys' fear is never realized until he is imprisoned or a fellow dope boy is killed. Thus, no one on the street listens when the convicted gives advice. The lessons that could be learned from a dope boy's eventual death gets lost in that "he was so young" sentiment thing.

Diddy was a high school dropout raised by a single parent. With two older brothers as his examples, Diddy became a part of the dope game that he knew very little about. No one properly taught his older brothers the dope game. Everything Diddy knew about the game was contrived in the alpha male syndrome of "see me." This "see me" approach to the game guaranteed the death, jail, or murder of Diddy, or the trick that was buying. In my opinion, this attitude of "I," "me," and "mine" has made the drug game so shallow that it's lost its purpose as a discrete business or its use as a way to make residual income for pimps.

I don't know if Diddy or his brothers have ever left the state of Georgia or wandered too far outside of their neighborhood. They'd just hangout in Fourth Ward wearing their long white T-shirts like a pack of wild dogs, looking to sell junk, whether good or bad, to a trick that was looking to buy. Unlike the dog pack, there was no leader or organization in Diddy's crowd, which consisted of his lukewarm friends. At least in a dog pack, there is only one dog that can wander about with his tail extended in the air. If another dog wants to wag his tail, then there is a fight between the two for domination and control. There is ultimately an understanding among the dogs — which one is the alpha male. So it goes, this analogy applies to the wolf, lion, hyena, and most other predators.

But, it does not apply to the unschooled street hustler.

See, there was no courtesy between Diddy and his friends of "I had the last trick so you can have this one." No, for Diddy and his pack, it was always who could make it to the trick's car first or who was the loudest or made the most noise and who was to be feared. To them, if you failed to participate on this level, you needed to pull your draws out of your ass and get on top of your game.

Diddy and his friends were just simple niggas without any finesse or smoothness about the game. They had no organization or plan to sell their merchandise. Lacking in collective or individual intelligent thought, they had no attorneys on board in case they were caught and they didn't have a relationship with police. Diddy and his friends were just niggas that sold from their momma's porch. They sold from their momma's porch because she needed the help. They sold from the porch because in her mind, she thought that nothing could happen to them if they sold it from home. Besides, she knew there was nothing she could do to stop them. Perhaps she liked the merchandise herself, so she allowed her boys to keep it close to her.

Diddy was never taught how to be a man among men because he never left his momma's porch. Trapped and unexposed to the world, Diddy lived in a vacuum, which made him as shallow as any client I had represented. Diddy either killed for sport or without reason. Even the most dangerous of all predators only kills for food or because it is threatened in its environment. Diddy allegedly killed the white dude because he chose a product other than Diddy's.

Diddy killed the dude around his friends. It was rumored that the piece used was involved in another murder or two separate and apart from Diddy's case. I thought that this was something that could be used when the time comes. But for now, all I could see was that Diddy was caught up in this "see me" thing. It's that "what do you think of me now" syndrome. It's a desire to make your peers see you as a crazy-ass gangster.

Diddy was trapped in a world where it was important for him to act in the way he thought he was perceived. If Diddy thought that people feared him, he would be the loud and bold one in the crowd. Diddy would walk around in the pack with his tail in the air because he was the crazy one, the alpha male. To solidify a reputation for himself, Diddy thought that if he would shoot someone, he would teach all future tricks that if you don't buy my shit, I will kill you.

Ultimately, Diddy just showed his friends that there was nothing decent about him. He was just young and ignorant to the ways of crime. He was a businessman who killed his customers. Diddy had never learned that if you are going to do something to someone, it was important to have a plan.

Basically, if you choose a life of crime, it's better and safer to do it by yourself — to walk alone. More importantly, Diddy had never learned that if you have to run away from the crime scene, then it ain't the right time. Diddy should have known that a young black man running down Boulevard is always suspicious. Thus, not only did his friends tell police on him, strangers identified the young black male running after they heard shots fired.

My brother, the former player, taught me lessons of the street my whole life. My brother would use these metaphors as he talked to me about life in the streets. One of his favorites was that water seeks it own level, meaning if you go into something, know your way out. Another one was, if your girl has a habit and it's not you, she's not for you. And, finally, if I ever ended up in prison or at a bar and things got out of hand, when in battle kill the noise first.

Real players had never schooled Diddy in the game. If they had, then Diddy would have known better than to shoot a man around eight of his friends and then run. Diddy, like so many wannabe players, was taught to sell his drugs from the front porch, wear a long oversized T-shirt uniform with pants falling off your ass and ride around on 24-inch rims in shiny cars advertising your trade. Neither Diddy nor his friends ever learned or understood discretion. Discretion for Diddy was hiding his drugs in his underwear. And, if Diddy really thought he was being smart, Diddy would hide his drugs underneath a brick about five feet from the curb in front of his house or wherever he and his friends were selling that day. As such, their ignorance is compounded by their lack of exposure and inability to express themselves to those outside of their neighborhoods.

When I lived in Chicago, I remember that the folks of the

crime-ridden Cabrini Green Housing Project were within walking distance to the celebrated Magnificent Mile in downtown Chicago, home to the great Oprah Winfrey and Phil Donohue Shows, which was one of Chicago's main tourist attractions.

Sadly, some folks from Cabrini Green were arrested by Chicago Police before ever setting foot on the Magnificent Mile. There were no security gates or roadblocks preventing the residents of Cabrini Green from visiting it. They just didn't feel comfortable enough in their own skin to venture out to see it. The Cabrini Green residents lived their life on a self-imposed plantation. I viewed Diddy and his friends in the Fourth Ward like the folks I met 20 years ago when I volunteered at the Cabrini Green Legal Aid Clinic.

Diddy's mother was in her mid-forties. She told me that her sons were in the streets and that I would get my money if I'd agree to represent Diddy. I gave her a shot and allowed her to pay me monthly. She eventually told me that she had resorted to selling fishplates over the weekends in her efforts to pay me. I asked her about her two older sons who promised to help pay for Diddy's legal fees. She told me that they didn't keep their promises to her. Even though it is illegal for me to accept known drug monies for attorney's fees, Diddy's momma had a square job, so I rationalized that whatever money she brought to me was cool.

I told her that I would resign from her baby's case if she continued to miss her monthly payments. I recalled how she begged and cried to me to give her more time. Diddy's grandmother then called me. She was on a fixed income. Grandma promised to send her social security check to me if I just stayed on to represent Diddy. With much reservation, I agreed to stay on. Grandma's check never came and neither did the money from the last fish fry, so I quit.

A young lady from the public defender's office was appointed to represent Diddy, so I gave her my file. She told me that she wasn't big on trial work like most trial attorneys, which I thought was odd because that's what public defenders do. However, at trial, she did the best that she could do for Diddy, considering all of his lukewarm friends who witnessed the shooting testified against him. At 19, Diddy was convicted of murder.

Sentence: Life in prison.

HONOR THY FATHER

"Honor thy father and thy mother: that thy days may be long upon the land that the Lord thy God giveth thee,"
Exodus 20:12

I stopped looking at dead pictures a long time ago. At first, to see a bloody crime scene was fascinating. To look at the dead and study it as an academic experience was something to talk about to friends and colleagues. But as you age, what was once youthful ignorance masked as professional curiosity becomes a grim reminder of your own mortality. You understand that the mind records everything it sees and that eventually you'll get tired of carrying the shit around in your mind. You may not be able to recall that particular piece of information or that one crime scene when you want to, but you will see it again and again for the rest of your life.

I don't know when I first started having dreams about crime scenes and pictures of dead people. It had to be around the time that I stopped looking at them. If someone didn't tell me they killed another in self-defense, I figured it was of no use to look at the pictures of dead people. I'd tell my client that if you weren't there at the time of the murder, who gives a fuck about the angles and trajectory of the bullets. Right, we weren't there so we didn't do it. As always, it was their risk to lie to me about what happened, even though I never really asked. I like to tell my client what his defense should be based on what I've read in the police reports. Besides, my version of the case always seems to find an out for the client.

I don't know why I ended up looking at these photos, but I did. At first, I would see them everyday for months on end in my mind. Then, I would see them every so often. I would see their faces when I was working out or taking a walk. I would see their faces even when I was fucking or getting my dick sucked. They were so young, sprawled out on the floor, bodies touching, and blood slippage inched out from one's head. Their eyes were open. Oh, they were so young. I don't think anyone chooses to die or be murdered in an abandoned house, but again, for the most part, only those that commit suicide chose where they die.

I don't know what it means to die a noble death anymore. Symbolically speaking, to die from old age doesn't necessarily mean one's death was noble anymore than a person who lived a noble life full of charity and was murdered. I guess I should resolve just to live in the extreme of being the best friend I could be, the best lover to as many women for as long as I can, and try to resolve it with God, such as Solomon did. I am no Solomon, but I trust that God will afford me the same judgment.

We live with the idea that we are not supposed to outlive our children. As parents, we are supposed to give our children the tools to make it in life. Lessons of God, integrity, loyalty, confidence, humbleness, and a sense of charity to prepare our children for the world. When those lessons are not passed down from generation to generation, something terrible happens, like the time I saw one of my five brothers smoking a joint with his teen-aged son, William.

When I came home from college, I would jog over to my brother's house. He lived about four miles from me. I'd usually run with a tank top on or no shirt at all, showing my ripped six-pack and broad shoulders and back. I would ask him when he was leaving the house or if he was coming over near my house. As if to imply, I wanted to double back and spend some quality time with his wife. This was my way of jokingly suggesting to him to keep his ass home. My brothers and I lived for the streets. As we had learned from our father, he lived for the weekend and that didn't include us.

On this occasion, I was angry with my brother for crossing the line of child-parent. Even though I did not have any kids, I knew that a parent should be a parent and not a friend to their kids. My brother's reasoning was that my nephew was a smoker and he would rather him smoke at home. Eventually, my brother died of a drug overdose, his widow became a crack user, and his son was killed in a drug-related murder.

Larry Hughes' story reminded me of my nephew, William. Larry was given up to $30,000 from his father to buy several kilos of cocaine. When Larry went to purchase the cocaine, he took his first cousin, Melvin Wilson. Melvin's mother and Larry's father were brother and sister. Larry and Melvin were ambushed and killed during the transaction. It's their pictures that I see in my sleep.

My client, Lil P, along with Bang, QT, and KT, was charged with killing Larry and his cousin Melvin. When I first met Lil P, he was fighting for his life. Someone had shot him twelve times and he was near death at the County Hospital. It was clear that Lil P's shooting was in retaliation. But I was impressed by the fact that Lil P never told authorities who shot him. Lil P had a medium brown complexion and stood about 5'10." He was still teenage skinny even though he was about 21 at the time of the murders.

Lil P wore tattoos all over his body, but the one I remembered most was the tattoo of the letter P in the middle of his forehead. His tattoos made Lil P look dirty to me. However, Lil P sported a nice smile and the ghetto girls loved him. I think he had fathered at least three kids that I knew of. Lil P's fashion sense would remind you of those out of Detroit — gold teeth and linen sets with gator shoes — "country cool."

Hughes was trying to buy three kilos of cocaine. I can only surmise that he was desperate to buy some cocaine because the last time he bought some from Bang, he had sold him some flex, which is fake cocaine. Hughes called Bang looking to buy. Bang didn't have any cocaine to sell, but he figured he could use the $30,000 he quoted Hughes for the coke. Bang then called Walter, a.k.a. Big Red, to teach him how to make a fake brick of cocaine. Big Red obliged and told Bang the ingredients that he needed, which included Arco starch, baking soda, etc.

Bang and KT commenced to cook the fake brick of cocaine. After they cooked it, they packaged it in newspaper and duct tape. Bang called Hughes and told him where to meet him. Hughes, being from the far Southside and not familiar with the ghetto right outside of downtown Atlanta, got lost. Some say Lil P went to pick him up from a neighborhood gas station where Hughes stopped and called for directions. Before Lil P allowed Hughes to follow him to the abandoned home, Bang had paid two junkies three dollars to leave the abandoned house. The house was one of those old shotgun houses I grew up in. Once you entered the front door, you could see all the way back to the kitchen door. The bedrooms were both on the right and left side of the hallway. Also, as you entered the house, there were stairs leading to the basement.

Hughes and Wilson had no idea where they were going, but I guess they thought they were prepared in case some shit jumped off. Both Hughes and Wilson had guns on them. In their minds, Bang was not going to flex Hughes again. Wilson, in fact, wore a holster with two guns and Hughes had his 9 mm in his pocket.

After Hughes and Wilson entered the house, Hughes showed QT and KT the money. QT showed Hughes and Wilson the coke. Hughes decided to unwrap the cocaine and test it. As Hughes tested the coke, it didn't take him long to find out that these niggas were trying to flex him again. They say that Hughes just gave Wilson a look and when Wilson attempted to pull out his gun, Bang exited from a closet by the stairs and shot Wilson through the heart. Wilson was ambushed. QT or KT then shot Hughes in the head as he attempted to raise his head from the table where he had tested the cocaine. Hughes managed to get off a round that got stuck in the wall before he was killed.

Wilson's and Hughes' bodies were then dragged and placed so that their bodies were touching. Bang, QT, or KT then removed the guns from their person and fled with their money. People say that Lil P was just the lookout, but Lil P did have his car painted just days after Hughes and Wilson were killed. Lil P said that was a coincidence and had nothing to do with the murders.

QT then told Big Red what happened and why they had to kill Hughes and Wilson. KT told his older brother pretty much the same story. Both Big Red and KT's brother told police on them niggas because they had unrelated cases and were selling information on for reduced time. QT was the first person arrested and he told on everybody. Bang and KT kept their mouth shut and refused to talk to police. Lil P was shot up in the hospital unable to talk. He was fighting for his life.

At first, the case was assigned to the Honorable Diva. We called her Diva because she was in fact a Diva. Diva was an Atlanta legend and one of the first black female judges in Atlanta. She understood the issues facing young black men. I say that because some judges don't understand nor do they even care. But in this case, no one really deserved any sympathy. These niggas were robbed and killed trying to buy some dope. Charge it to the game. That's what happens when you pick up a hot pot. You get burned.

With heels, Diva was almost 6-feet tall. She had a caramel complexion and a full mane of hair that fell to her shoulders. If Diva had a weakness, it was strong black men. If you asked the Diva for something with conviction, chances are she'd give it to you. I don't know if this applied in her personal life. I knew of at least four husbands.

I've been around long enough to know, that if Lil P went to trial with a nigga named Bang, he would be convicted. I heard that Bang got his name earnestly as in "Bang Bang you're dead." QT and KT were no better. Both had extensive criminal histories for selling cocaine. Lil P had a few convictions, but he was really small-time compared to Bang, QT, and KT. Besides, Lil P was merely a look-out, if that.

I convinced Diva to sever our case from Bang, QT, and KT. I told Diva that the crackheads knew Lil P. Moreover, the crackheads all agreed that it was QT, Bang, and KT who paid them the three dollars to use the house. However, the crackheads didn't mention anything about Lil P to police. I reasoned that they didn't mention Lil P because he wasn't there. Diva agreed with me and severed Lil P from the trial. Besides, no one wanted to roll Lil P's hospital bed into the court room or wait on Lil P to recover from his wounds before we could start the trial. Thus, when the time came, Lil P was to have his own trial.

What's always sad to me is when young men decide to kill each other. QT, KT, and Bang had already decided to kill Hughes and Wilson if they learned the drugs were flex. Conversely, Wilson and Hughes had decided to do the same.

The question for me was when did Hughes' father decide to sacrifice him? Most of us remember the story of Abraham when God instructed him to kill his own son Isaac to show his faith in God. What was particularly sadistic to me was that Abraham just couldn't kill his son on the spot. He had to travel three days to a specific location at the foot of a mountain. Over the course of those three days, Abraham reminisced about the lessons and stories he had shared with Isaac. Abraham thought about the moments of Isaac's birth and questions of curiosity Isaac had asked Abraham as a boy. For three days, as Abraham and Isaac walked to the mountain, Abraham thought about the fact he was about to sacrifice his own son to show obedience to his Lord.

I thought why was Hughes' father sacrificing him, for money? We know the only thing that comes from living the life of selling drugs is prison or death. As a community of lawyers, we have become numb to the inevitable outcome of kids that live the dope boy life. We know that to attach ourselves to this kid will one day result in a bad personal experience for us. In many ways, we have given up on the young dope boys because we don't have anything attractive enough to offer them. We have nothing to bring them back to the square life. So, dope boys continue to litter our prisons and graveyards.

Some of my colleagues hold out hope that the dope boys will change, like many of my colleagues who changed after they learned their cocaine habit was bigger than them. Like my older brother who learned the same thing after his cocaine-induced heart attack changed him. Hence, we all know where we came from and change can happen. I can't think of any good reason why Hughes' father sacrificed him like my brother sacrificed his son, William.

The case took four years before it went to trial. By this time, Lil P had had 12 surgeries from the twelve gunshot wounds he'd received. When Bang, QT, and KT went to trial, Lil P still had the shit bag coming from his side. Of course, Hughes' father never showed up for the trial. I guess him not showing up was not because it was too painful. But, instead, I think he was afraid of being arrested and charged with his own son's murder. Georgia has some weird laws on conspiracy to sell or buy cocaine when someone gets killed.

Futhermore, I never met Lil P's father either. I think his mother died when he was a child, but he loved his grandmother, and that was a good thing. Perhaps Lil P could love her enough to get out of the game and live a square life. You know, love her enough to change if not for her, at least for his kids.

It was almost funny how KT's girlfriend Wanda, testified that KT was with her at the time of the murder. "Him didn't do it, him with me." I don't know if this is exactly what she said, it's just that I've heard this statement so much over the past umpteen years from Chicago to Atlanta, it doesn't matter. It's just what I hear, "him didn't do it. Him with me." She told the jury that she and KT were bowling. Moreover, they went bowling nearly every weekend for the past five years. However, when asked by the prosecutor where the bowling alley was located, she didn't know the address. What made matters even worse, she told the prosecutor that KT had bowled a 500, everyone in the courtroom laughed. As she prepared for trial, it seemed like KT's lawyer should have told her that 300 was the maximum score in the sport of bowling.

Wanda's testimony was as bad as smelly fish and as convincing as one that could talk. The police used QT's statement to convict him. Bang was probably convicted because he sat at the trial and didn't say anything. Most people know that you have a right not to testify, but at what point do you say to an accuser, " I didn't kill them or I did kill them because they were going to kill me." Consequently, Bang's and KT's asses were convicted.

The judge sentenced Bang, QT, and KT to two consecutive life sentences or as we say in the business, two nickels. A friend of mine, Walter represented Bang. I know that Walter begged Bang to testify. Walter believed that if he could show the jury that there was a shootout because Hughes or Wilson had fired their gun, he could get Bang a lesser sentence; 20 years opposed to two nickels. Bang refused. To the contrary, the prosecutor theorized that it was Wilson that squeezed out a shot as he was being shot and that Hughes never had a chance to fire.

Today, when I see Walter, I introduce him as the lawyer who got his client two nickels. As if to say, his client would have been better off representing himself. Walter, in turn, introduces me as the attorney whose client got the death penalty in an unrelated case. Whenever he says this about me, I find myself explaining. Firstly, my client wasn't put to death and secondly, he knows that I resigned from that client's case before anything was resolved.

I asked family and friends whether a child must honor thy father in all circumstances. My friend Walter, who represented Bang was a preacher's kid. Walter told me that honoring thy father simply means to respect him, not to obey his crazy ass.

Lil P's case was dismissed.

THE CLEAN UP MEN OF CAIRO

Here I am again in my bathroom mirror trying to make sense out of what now has become the new nigga shit. How do you explain to somebody that your client is accused of kidnapping and torturing someone who is found dead in the trunk of a car? Moreover, after the guy died, your client and others cut his body up into nine pieces with a chainsaw and buried him about town. How do you explain all of this to a jury and keep a straight face?

I figured, however, if I could explain it to myself, I could explain it to a jury. As always, I found that the easiest way to approach this dilemma would be to blame it on someone else. So I did.

I would tell the jury that this case was called "The Clean-Up Men Of Cairo." Although this case had nothing to do with Egypt or Africa, Cairo is simply a street in Northwest Atlanta. At 1052 Cairo Street, the Kelley's had a well-known, family-run crack cocaine trap. In November of 2001, someone stole $75,000 worth of cocaine.

This was a case of the kidnapping, torture, and murder of the person the Kelley's thought stole their dope, their cousin Deke the

Freak. I told the jury that throughout this trial, they would not find the murderers of Deke on trial. But instead, that they would only hear from the men who cleaned up afterwards, if you believed them. I shared with the jury that I did not.

Coming into the trial, I knew what I was dealing with. I figured that if I could just explain to the jury what type of motherfuckers the state had as witnesses, my guy would have a shot at walking. See, not only did I know what I was dealing with, I knew who I was dealing with even though I had never met any of the players personally. I only had the mug shots and criminal histories of these dudes. But on the other hand, I knew that everyone involved was a nigga or had some nigga in him.

Since I had met niggas before, I felt comfortable enough in my skills to explain the difference between black folks and niggas to the jury. I had a distinct advantage over the other lawyers in the case. Not that I was the only black lawyer, but my advantage was that I use to be a nigga myself. Not that I was raised that way, but for many years I was a nigga by choice. And then I decided to be black.

It helped that I had a jury of at least five or six blacks. I made the assumption that they may have known or had past experiences with niggas as well, but I wasn't sure. I had to take a chance. Chris Rock once told Ed Bradley of 60 Minutes that he loves black people but he can't stand niggas. Rock went on to say that a nigga would steal your TV and then sell it back to you. Or as in our case, cut Deke's head off and bury it. Then make a deal with the state for no or reduced charges to rat out the other perpetrators. Sadly, the state struck such a deal with K.B., Fabu, and Scooby Doo in the drug-related chainsaw murder of Deke the Freak.

The cast of characters in this case included as many as eight defendants, all charged with murder and kidnapping. At first glance, I couldn't believe what I was reading. Black folks just didn't do stuff like this. This genre of murder was mafia shit usually found in Chicago, Philly, or New York by others, but not by black folks.

Indicted were C-Bo, who had never been found or arrested and, by all accounts, the ringleader of the family business; brothers Big-T and his younger brother Hootie, Bullet Proof, Fabu, Scooby Doo, Dread, and Mark Anthony, the only Puerto Rican in the family.

Anthony, the Puerto Rican, told a girlfriend that he had shot Deke as he tried to escape from Big-T's truck over on Cairo. The girlfriend offered this information in exchange for a reduction in her jail sentence on an unrelated matter. Her plan backfired when the medical examiner found no bullet holes or casings in Deke's badly decomposed body.

After this discovery, the state dropped the murder charges on Mark Anthony and Dread. Mark Anthony still didn't leave jail. He's doing time for cocaine trafficking in an unrelated matter, anyway. In 2000, it was also rumored that Anthony may have been involved with the assassination of the sheriff in a different town, but he was never charged.

Big-T was a Morehouse graduate from Nashville and he was a football player. Big-T had a fair complexion and was about 6'3," 300 pounds, shaved head and well spoken. If any one of the defendants had any redeeming qualities, it was Big-T, the Pee Wee football coach.

Big-T was represented by Gilligan. Gilligan was this Southern Baptist dude who had more insecurities than any kept woman that I have ever met. Gilligan was a frumpy non-athletic looking dude who wore the same wrinkled blue jacket and khakis to trial everyday. Sometimes he looked like he had slept in his clothes and just rolled on into court. Gilligan also wore some dusty old hush puppies with sloped heels that forced his ankles to slightly bulge over his shoes.

Gilligan was the prototype public defender, with his wire-rimmed glasses and sweaty palms. He seemed scared shitless to be at the defense table on such a case. But I think his fear drove him to meticulously prepare for trial. Gilligan was ready. Big-T, however, couldn't stand him.

Gilligan had a habit of asking for your opinion on his every move, while violating all the rules of personal space. He would constantly push his glasses up and if you yelled or even slightly raised your voice at him, he'd become extremely apologetic. Not the type of guy you'd want fighting for your life. Sometimes he'd appear to be so nervous you'd think he was going to wet himself. On a rare occasion when he would make a valid point, he needed instant approval, like a puppy that just learned a new trick and wanted a treat.

I represented Hootie, who was Big-T's younger brother. They had the same mother but different fathers. He was a small dude, brown, 5'8," 150 pounds, hustler. Hootie had an open gun case pending in Federal Court in Nashville for gun running. Supposedly, he was only here in Atlanta to take Big-T back to Nashville for Thanksgiving. Before they could leave deservingly or not, he and Big-T got caught up in this murder and couldn't get out of Atlanta for good without standing trial for it.

Hootie's and Big-T's mother called me once and wanted to know what was going on. I told her what the allegations were. She told me nothing from her could do what had been alleged. She told me Hootie was her baby and that she needed to trust me. I told her she could and that I would do my best. She also told me not to do anything to hurt Big-T. I said nothing to this because in my mind, Big-T was to be the sacrifice for Hootie. As far as my strategy was concerned, Big-T was guilty as hell anyway.

For whatever reason, Hootie called me Skipper. From time to time, Hootie and Big-T would nudge me to object for Gilligan. They'd say, "Come on Skipper, help him out." Earlier in the trial, I sat there and minded my own business. However, as the trial progressed, I found myself trying to represent them both.

Bullet Proof was a convicted felon with one murder already to his credit. He served 10 years in prison on that murder, after the state reduced it to manslaughter. Bullet Proof had a brown complexion and was about 6'1," 280 pounds. He sported some healed, visible scars about his face and he was mustached. This was a real

Ving Rhymes/Charles Dutton type. But he was no actor. He was a convicted killer and everyone in the courtroom knew it.

To me, Bullet Proof appeared to have been fearless and not to be fucked with under any circumstances. One morning, he spoke to me and I told him to suck on a few of them motherfuckin' mints before he spoke to me. The other defendants were alarmed at my comment to Bullet Proof. I told him just like Bernie Mac, "Nigga, I ain't scared of ya," and we all laughed after Bullet Proof did.

I believe that Bullet Proof was the type of dude who would kick his own mother's ass if he thought she was slacking when she fixed his plate. Bullet Proof appeared to be a real unrepented, unapologetic criminal. Up until this time, I had only met about five of these sociopath types. He was definitely number six.

The Professor represented Bullet Proof. The Professor was a brother who graduated from Stanford. He was a great orator, but he was more passionate about his writing. A real lawyer, he'd practice law by day but by night, he'd write his legal publication. The Professor had at one time worked as an assistant district attorney in Atlanta. Rumor had it that he was forced to resign after he dropped murder charges against a dude. In that case, the Professor thought his witnesses were lying. I always admired the Professor for having the balls to make such a move.

Bullet Proof needed nothing less than the Professor as his lawyer. During the trial, I never saw the Professor or Bullet Proof greet one another. I'm not saying they didn't; I just didn't see it.

A Cuban lawyer who was intellectually quick and a very sharp dresser represented Scooby Doo. The Cuban was truly a shark in the courtroom and would take no prisoners. Interestingly enough, the Cuban spent his spare time in South Africa working on their National Constitution. He truly had a revolutionary spirit and was more committed to the cause of the disenfranchised than anyone else in the case. After Scooby made a deal to testify against the others, Scooby was cut loose by the state. Still, the Cuban would show up in court everyday. I don't know how he convinced the

District Attorney's Office to cut guilty-ass Scooby a deal, but he did.

Fabu, which was short for Fabulous, was a self-proclaimed schizophrenic. Deke suffocated in the trunk of Fabu's car. Fabu wore these long, beautiful black dread locks, which offended me. Dreads are supposed to represent a oneness with God. A way of life that is wholesome and clean. Today, it's simply a matter of style for both men and women. Like everything else, dreads have lost their meaning. Dreads now have false prophets, just like my Christians.

Fabu not only participated in the kidnapping of Deke, he helped dismember and dispose of the body, with C-Bo, Scooby, and K.B. After he was arrested, Fabu turned into a state's witness after promising the state that he would help them find C-Bo. He claimed he was the only person that C-Bo would trust. Fabu and C-Bo were childhood friends and have known each other their whole lives. C-Bo trusted him because he wasn't as deep in the game as the others. As a condition of Fabu's release, he had to testify truthfully. I imagined that Fabu would say anything to keep his ass out of jail for life — I would. Fabu received probation for his role in Deke's murder.

Yeah, it's true, the kidnapped victim died in the trunk of Fabu's car, was then cut up into nine pieces with a chainsaw, and buried in various locations in Atlanta. And the kidnapper/murderer received probation. This only happens in Hollywood and Atlanta, but at least in Hollywood you have to be a celebrity with money to get away with murder.

Ginger represented Fabu. I called her Ginger because she reminded me of the Ginger on Gilligan's Island. Ginger had natural blonde hair and blue eyes. She was as thin as a rail. She was a white man's fantasy. Ginger spoke with the true gentility of southern charm, reminding one of a different time. Sometimes I would intentionally engage her in conversation using every four-letter word I could, just to see how she would respond. Ginger never blushed. I'm sure she thought I was an ill-mannered bag of wind who talked more than a crackhead at a crime scene.

Ginger lived in an area where they still proudly displayed the Confederate flag on their homes, businesses, and cars. I could only imagine a dread walking into an office building with the Confederate flag draped over the door. However, I can't be too judgmental of Fabu. He hired the best his money could buy to avoid spending the rest of his life in prison. Shit, if Bill Duke, the notorious Klansman was a lawyer and he was the best my money could buy, fuck the Confederate flag, I'll cook that bitch's lunch. Besides, Ginger didn't appear to be a racist to me. Ginger was a lawyer who got a hell of a deal for a murderer.

K.B. was the facilitator or second in command to C-Bo. If C-Bo wanted something done, he would call K.B. K.B. was the type of nigga that all southern blacks and whites alike hated. He was that crooked northern nigga from New Jersey who thought everyone in the South was stupid. Transplants like me are embarrassed of the K.B.'s in Atlanta. It's like taking a relative somewhere who doesn't know how to eat, but draws attention to himself because he's so loud.

K.B. was the type of opportunistic thug that was probably run out of New Jersey. The type of thug that if he caught you sleeping at the wheel, he felt that it was his duty to rob, steal, or otherwise fuck with you. K.B. was also dating C-Bo's younger sister, Missy.

A little man, K.B. spent his time in prison pumping iron. He was tattooed and for the most part a living cliché. For example, he was the prison dude who tried to use adjectives he wasn't used to using. He was the type of dude who would tell police you were hiding in a tree when he was caught hiding in the bushes. "Come on out man, they caught us."

K.B. was never indicted or arrested for Deke's kidnapping and murder. See, K.B. went to the police first. In the criminal game, it's an unwritten rule that no matter what you do, if you get on the bus first you get the best deal. So it goes, a guy could hire another guy to kill someone. The guy does. The first one to the police with information about the murder could walk away scot-free. Indeed, this is exactly what happened in our case.

K.B. was the first on the bus. He told his story to Det. Rodriquez, of the Atlanta Police Department. Det. Rodriquez was a fairly new dick who did nothing to verify what he was told by K.B. Seemingly, Det. Rodriquez took everything K.B. told him at face value.

Det. Rodriquez was of Spanish decent and had Hollywood looks. His slender, athletic build suggested he was a runner. At first, I thought Det. Rodriquez had one or two obvious character flaws. He was either naive or lazy. It would take some time to figure exactly which one he was. As the case unfolded, it didn't take too long to figure out what was going on. Decisions were made during the trial that were out of his control. He made it a point to let me know this. He told me he can put the case together, but he can't try the damn thing. However, this would not be the last time Rodriquez and I would dance.

K.B. told Det. Rodriquez a story that went something like this: Some time in November, K.B. placed $75,000 worth of cocaine in the common drop-off point for C-Bo to pick up later. The drop-off point was inside the trunk of an old non-working car in Deke's mother's yard.

Deke and C-Bo were cousins. C-Bo wanted Deke to be in the family cocaine business, but Deke refused. Even though Deke worked every day, Deke's thing was to steal cocaine from the dope boys off Cairo Street. I don't mean to confuse anyone. Deke was no Robin Hood. Deke stole for Deke. After the cocaine was stolen, the shakedown began.

C-Bo apparently got the coke on consignment from Doughboy. Doughboy was one of the biggest drug dealers in Atlanta. Doughboy would buy directly from the Colombians. Thus, Doughboy had to pay the Colombians for the coke or Doughboy would have been tortured and dismembered himself. Since shit rolls downhill, Doughboy was giving C-Bo time to make it right before the Colombians got impatient.

C-Bo and K.B. first shook down Scooby Doo and then this guy named Dread. A few days later, they jacked up a third guy called Ying-Yang before they focused on "Deke the Freak." It was never really made clear to me why they turned to Deke. Other than his stellar reputation of stealing niggas' coke, C-Bo had nothing really to go on. However, C-Bo did notice after the coke was stolen Deke stopped coming around Cairo Street. Before, Deke would only receive little retribution if caught stealing from others. See, Deke knew who to steal from and he was C-Bo's cousin. Everybody around Cairo Street was afraid of C-Bo.

Like Bullet Proof, C-Bo was a real killer and had been convicted of trafficking in cocaine when this shit went down. After a jury convicted C-Bo, a trusting judge allowed him two weeks to get his affairs in order. Facing 20 years in prison, C-Bo fled. That little move of C-Bo's really fucked it up for everybody. Today, the trusting judge is ordering motherfuckers and their cousins to jail immediately after conviction, two at a time.

K.B. claimed Deke heard that C-Bo was desperate and was questioning everyone in or out of the game about the stolen coke. Eventually, C-Bo thought Deke was avoiding him. This belief turned C-Bo's suspicion into action to find Deke.

Deke had a nice house in Norcross, a northern suburb of Atlanta, and no one really knew where he lived. Strangely enough, after the coke was stolen, Deke wasn't even coming over to Cairo to visit his own momma. When he missed Sunday dinner, C-Bo was convinced Deke had stolen his dope. See, Deke and C-Bo always grabbed a plate at big momma's house on Sundays.

When Deke missed Sunday dinner, C-Bo had his younger brother, Lil-Bo, to lure Deke over to the dope house. The dope house was right next door to where the dope was stolen. Lil-Bo told Deke he had some fire-ass weed that he had to check out and Deke came through. When Deke walked through the door, he asked if C-Bo was around. Lil-Bo told him no. Quietly, C-Bo was waiting in the den. When Deke walked through to the den, C-Bo was waiting with his shit in his hand; they said it was a 9 mm.

C-Bo then summoned for Big-T, who within minutes pulled in front of Lil-Bo's house in a black Expedition. C-Bo and Big-T took Deke the Freak over to Ying-Yang's house where they stripped him down to his underwear and duct-taped his hands and feet. C-Bo and the others began to beat Deke's ass to make sure everybody had a part. K.B. claimed that Deke's ass whipping was already in progress when he got to Ying-Yang's house. K.B. said that Big-T, C-Bo, Ying-Yang, Lil-Bo, Dread, Scooby Doo, and Doughboy were all present at Ying-Yang's house during the first beating.

Later that morning, K.B. said that C-Bo decided to take Deke to his dope house over in the Bluff. This house is about three miles from Cairo Street. K.B. said that the intent was to beat Deke's ass some more when they got there. Deke, being true to himself, called the whole family a bunch of bitch-ass niggas. Deke even called Big-T soft, which everybody thought was funny since Big-T is the big ball player. Big-T promised Deke he would show him just how soft he really was after they got to the Bluff.

As they got ready to leave Ying-Yang's apartment, K.B. placed a bag over Deke's head. K.B. said he led Deke down the stairs and placed Deke in Big-T's truck. Big-T and C-Bo set out to transport Deke over to the Bluff. Just as they made it there, Deke jumped out of the truck in his draws and attempted to escape. Deke began banging on people's doors, running and screaming for help. This occurred at about five o'clock Monday morning.

A concerned citizen saw and heard Deke banging on her door, but understandably, she would not open the same. She told the jury she cautiously approached her door, but intentionally left the light off. She was afraid because she lives alone and doesn't own a gun. After observing Deke through her front window and the men pursuing him, she called police. She also told police that she heard a gunshot strike her house. She gave a description of two people that resembled Big-T and C-Bo chasing Deke.

An 80-year-old newspaper deliveryman observed two dudes

chasing Deke. The old man said Deke grabbed him and pleaded for help as the big, light-skinned guy and a dark, bald guy put him back in the SUV at gunpoint. The old man said that the big, light-skinned guy was very nice, but he had on a torn shirt. As they left, the old man noticed that Deke's blood was on one of the newspapers. He gave the paper to police.

Deke was taken to the Bluff and kept there for most of the day. There, C-Bo put a fierce-ass whipping on Deke for trying to escape. Repeatedly, C-Bo would put a plastic bag over Deke's head until he couldn't breathe and then he would take it off. This went on for several hours until C-Bo got tired. A weary Deke then offered to help C-Bo find the coke. But, Deke still claimed he didn't have it.

That night, Deke was transported to Betty Crocker's house for a Monday night football party. Betty lived in a southern suburb of Atlanta with her kids. Betty's son played on the same team as C-Bo's son. Betty stated they barbecued and C-Bo had K.B. bring some chicken from the chicken shack off Old National Highway. K.B. claimed he took Hootie, Scooby Doo, and Deke some chicken. During the game, Hootie and Scooby Doo stayed in Big-T's truck and watched Deke.

I knew K.B. was lying about Hootie because Betty said these guys were at her house for hours. Betty stated she never met or saw anyone named Hootie. Also, in K.B.'s original statement to Det. Rodriquez, he never mentioned anything about Hootie. K.B. had forgotten about Hootie and now he had to tie up the loose ends.

Betty did see Big-T, who showed up after everybody else. To her, Big-T appeared to be wearing a T-shirt that was too small for him. When Betty asked Big-T about the shirt, he gave her some bullshit about him tearing his shirt somehow. During the game, Betty claimed she also saw Fabu, Scooby, and K.B., but no Deke.

Later on that Monday night, Deke ended up in the trunk of Fabu's car. Fabu claimed he didn't know anything about this. He further claimed that C-Bo later apologized to him for instructing K.B. to put Deke into the trunk of his car. After the game, the party went further south to C-Bo's sister's house.

Sister-Bo had two teenage daughters and an ill aunt living with her. When C-Bo arrived, she claimed she was asleep and bed-ridden from a recent hysterectomy. C-Bo and Big-T came into her room and asked to spend the night. She told them no. She thought they had left, but she saw C-Bo the next morning when she woke up. However, Big-T must have left.

Later that night, Sister-Bo saw Scooby, K.B., and Fabu at her house. Her two daughters saw the same guys and Dread. In fact, neither daughter saw Bullet Proof, Big-T, or Hootie that night or the following day. The daughters even denied seeing Big T's Expedition parked in their yard during that time. The girls did, however, see a U-Haul truck parked in their driveway.

Amazingly, neither Sister-Bo nor her daughters heard a chainsaw in their basement. I figured they must sleep just as hard as both my big ass and my cousin Ruth, who was a severe asthmatic.

K.B. said he did not initially go over to Sister-Bo's house. He claimed that as he was driving home on I-20, when Fabu called him. Fabu had summoned him back to the house because Deke would not quiet down in the trunk. Fabu informed K.B. that Deke was flopping around, making a lot of noise, and pleading to get out of the trunk of the car. Before K.B. could turn around, he received another call from C-Bo instructing him to meet O'jay at the gas station off of I-20 and Hill Street to pick up a chainsaw.

Upon returning with the chainsaw, K.B. gave it to C-Bo. K.B. then claimed C-Bo took Deke out of the trunk of Fabu's car and took him inside Sister-Bo's house, straight to the basement. K.B. claimed that C-Bo, Big-T, Hootie, Scooby Doo, and Fabu were all there when he returned with the chainsaw.

To the contrary, Fabu claimed he left Sister-Bo's house after K.B. took Deke out of the trunk of his car. Fabu claimed it was K.B. and not C-Bo who took Deke out of the trunk. I really didn't give a damn who took Deke out of the car so long as it wasn't Hootie.

Fabu went on to say that before he left, C-Bo promised him he would fix the trunk light that Deke fucked up. K.B. and Fabu both claimed that Deke was still alive when they left Sister-Bo's house.

K.B. said that the following Tuesday morning, he received a call from C-Bo. C-Bo instructed him to bring some garbage bags and come over to the house. When he got there, he saw a U-Haul truck parked by the garage. As K.B. entered the house, he observed C-Bo, Big-T, Hootie, and Scooby in the basement. However, K.B. did not see Deke. K.B. said C-Bo took the bags and they began removing body parts from the herby kirby (garbage container with wheels) and placing them in the bags.

K.B. said the bags he brought were too small, so he and C-Bo went to the depot store and bought some bigger bags. When they returned, everyone started putting body parts in the bags. K.B. observed that Deke had been cut at the joints. His arms and legs were severed from the torso. Each hand was cut off at the wrist and I think, but I'm not sure, they may have even cut his feet off. Deke's head was severed at the neck. As K.B. was taking it all in, Big-T asked K.B. what the fuck he was looking at because he wasn't helping. K.B. began to help place the body parts into thc bags.

After they put the body parts in the bags, they put the bags back into the herby kirby and set it inside the U-Haul. C-Bo instructed everyone to disrobe and put their clothes in a bag. C-Bo then put that bag of clothes on the truck as well.

K.B., Scooby, and Fabu drove the truck over to K.B.'s apartment to wait for further instructions from C-Bo. En route, the herby kirby tipped over and Deke's body parts and blood spilled into the truck. K.B. told C-Bo they needed to torch the truck but C-Bo wouldn't okay it. They were going to have to just bleach it out when K.B. got to his apartment.

K.B. lived in an eastern suburb about 30 miles from Sister-Bo. Within an hour after K.B. parked the truck, suspicious cops started checking the truck out. They checked the Vehicle Identification Number to see if it was stolen before they were called away. In a quiet moment, Scooby and K.B. drove the truck over to Maple's house, who was one of K.B.'s women. Somewhere between K.B.'s apartment and Maple's house, K.B. threw the clothes in a dumpster.

Maple was a teacher's assistant in a suburban school district. She and K.B. had dated on and off for a while, but I'm not sure when or how they met. K.B. asked Maple to use her freezer. He promised her a new freezer for her old one. She asked no questions and was excited about the promise of a new freezer. I thought to myself, do you really know who's teaching your kids?

K.B. and Scooby removed the body parts from the herby kirby and placed them in the freezer. They noticed they had all the body parts with the exception of the head. They thought they had lost it or left it in Sister-Bo's basement. Panicked and concerned, they called C-Bo and told him they didn't have the head. C-Bo told them it was cool. He kept Deke's head for himself.

Hours later C-Bo then called a meeting at a pool room on the East side of Atlanta. K.B. brought Maple to the meeting because he couldn't take a chance on her looking inside the freezer. Maple recalled seeing C-Bo, Scooby, Fabu, Bullet Proof, and some other guys at the meeting. Maple did not see Big-T or Hootie. C-Bo instructed K.B., Scooby, and Fabu to find two different locations to bury Deke's body parts and they did. Being unsatisfied with the locations, C-Bo found a place on his own. Thereafter, C-Bo returned to the spot with Scooby and Fabu and instructed them to dig the grave, and they did.

On Wednesday, Maple observed K.B., Scooby, and Bullet Proof remove her freezer and place it on the U-Haul. K.B. and Scooby left Maple's house and drove around I-285 until they received further instructions from C-Bo. K.B. decided to go buy some weed, so he stopped at a place in Decatur. As he pulled in to the lot, two dudes tried to rob them. K.B. was shot in the hand. Scooby took over the wheel and dropped K.B. off at Grady Hospital. Scooby couldn't stay off course. Deke's body parts are still on the truck. Later that night after K.B. got out of the hospital, he, Scooby, Fabu, C-Bo, and others buried Deke's body parts in Atlanta and Dekalb County. Since

K.B.'s hand was fucked up, he was the lookout.

Then, it was time for K.B. to return the truck. He and Scooby had scrubbed it down with bleach at Maple's house after they had placed the body parts in the freezer. While en route to return the truck, they stopped and burned the herby kirby and chainsaw in a vacant lot. A few days later, Scooby, K.B., Fabu, and C-Bo buried Deke's head in a park in Atlanta. By this time, Big-T and Hootie had taken off and returned to Nashville.

Within a few weeks of Deke's unceremonious burial, Deke's wife and sister, Elvira, started their own investigation. While violating all rules of police work, they stumbled across information that they gave to Det. Rodriquez. This information proved to be Rodriquez's first solid lead in to Deke's disappearance.

See, Deke's wife and Elvira kidnapped and duct-taped C-Bo's younger brother, Lil-Bo. Lil-Bo was the one who lured Deke over to his house to buy some weed before he was kidnapped. Elvira threatened to kill Lil-Bo if he didn't give them some information on who drove the black Expedition. Elvira was Lil-Bo's own cousin. Elvira had her own unrelated murder case pending and she told Lil-Bo another one wouldn't make much difference to her. Everyone on Cairo Street knew not to fuck with Elvira. They knew that Elvira was just as deep in the game as anybody else.

Within minutes, Lil-Bo told on Big-T. Deke's wife passed this information on to Det. Rodriquez. Det. Rodriquez then put the word on the street that they were looking for Big-T. Shortly thereafter, K.B. received a call from C-Bo to get rid of Big-T's truck. K.B. was dropped off at Big-T's Cobb County address and drove Big-T's truck over to C-Bo's mechanic in Dekalb County, about 40 minutes East of Cobb.

Det. Rodriquez then secured a warrant for Big-T's arrest. When police had made it to Big-T's home, they claimed it had been abandoned. Also, there were several malnourished pitbulls that were starving or had died on his property.

K.B. instructed the mechanic to remove the engine from the

truck. As the mechanic removed the engine, he finds blood in the truck and panics. The mechanic then contacts C-Bo and demands that the truck be removed immediately. After a few days, K.B. has the truck towed to a secluded location. There, K.B. paid a crack-head to torch the truck.

Eventually, Nashville Police arrested Big-T on the warrant from Atlanta and held him for questioning in Deke's disappearance. Moreover, Hootie had an outstanding warrant for gun running in Nashville, so they both were arrested from their mother's home. It would be the last time they would see their mother alive.

A week later, a kid was arrested after leading police on a high-speed chase, driving Deke's car. He's eventually caught and interviewed. He tells Det. Rodriquez that he got the car from Scooby Doo, a dude that hangs out around Cairo Street. K.B. heard someone was popped driving Deke's car. Apparently, when K.B. told Scooby to get rid of the car, the motherfucker rented the car for some crack. K.B., seeing shit unravel, ran to the police and got complete immunity in exchange for his testimony against Big-T, Hootie, Bullet Proof, C-Bo, and the others.

As with every case that involves the proverbial stool pigeon, you look for witnesses who are not a part of the game. In our case, we had an 80-year-old newspaper man, a concerned citizen, Sister-Bo, and her daughters, Betty Crocker and Maple. Luckily for Hootie, none of these people identified him.

We selected a jury that included a lady who was a college Professor at Spelman. She had also run for mayor of Atlanta on two occasions and lost. This lady was by trade an economist, and the academic superior to our current mayor.

For us, however, the mayor that never was became essential to our jury because Spelman College is the sister School of Morehouse College. We felt if anyone would save Big-T, it would be her. We felt the other jurors would follow her lead. Even though, she was not the foreperson. She was clearly the dominant personality we needed.

Our judge was an experienced jurist who didn't take any shit.

She reminded me of Robin Williams in Ms. Doubtfire. She was the type of judge that when she took the bench, she had to restrain herself from cussing out lawyers who, in her opinion, talked too much. She handled her share of the high-profile cases that came through Atlanta. She was direct and irritable to both the prosecutors and the defense attorneys.

The trial began and we were on for a two-week fuck-fest. Professor and I couldn't agree on a common theory, so we agreed as gentlemen not to hurt each other's client, if possible. Big-T kept tugging on my suit coat asking me "Don't fuck with me." I lied to him and told him I wouldn't so he would stop begging and pouring my water and shit.

I went into the trial with the intent of throwing muddy hog shit on K.B., C-Bo, Fabu, and Scooby before asking any questions. I felt it important to create the mood for the trial. The plan was to spare Big-T and Bullet Proof depending on if the newspaper man and the concerned citizen held up as credible witnesses. Everyone knew that Hootie was the only real outsider, since he still lived in Nashville and had only visited Atlanta on two occasions.

As we were about to start, Gilligan wanted to have a hearing on what photos the state should not be allowed to use. Gilligan argued that the glossy 10" x 10" photos of a decomposed head with skin slippage would shock the jury so much they would convict everybody for the hell of it. Judge Doubtfire agreed. She excluded all the morbid photos of Deke's wet head and body parts being excavated by police.

Judge Doubtfire also kept out other autopsy photos that were even worse than the excavation pictures. As it was, Gilligan and the wrinkled suit had come to play and faired well for Big-T early on in the trial.

K.B. was one of the first witnesses to testify. By this time, he had given four different statements to police and led them to Deke's body. I couldn't wait to question him on how he described what happened to Deke in his statement to Det. Rodriquez. K.B. told him that, "After they cut the nigga up, I helped put his ass in the Herby Kirby." Det. Rodriquez himself was so taken back with K.B.'s cold and nonchalant description of Deke's death that he reminded K.B. that his statement was being videotaped.

To the jury, that statement alone was enough to know who was talking to them. K.B., being such a small man, I asked him if he'd fetch anything C-Bo told him to. Knowing this would piss him off, K.B. told me that dogs fetched and he was no dog. I said you fetched the chicken for the football game, you fetched the chainsaw, you fetched the garbage bags, and you fetched Big-T's truck. K.B. told me he was helping out a friend.

I reminded him that between the time of Deke's murder and this trial, he had married C-Bo's younger sister, Missy. K.B. all but told me that he didn't need me to remind him whom he was married. But with that bit of information, the jury had every reason to suspect that K.B. still had C-Bo's best interest at heart. Conversely, he did not give a shit about Big-T, Hootie, and Bullet Proof. Finally, I then asked K.B. why did he kill Deke? K.B. then said to the jury — looking as sincere as the nigga he was — that he didn't kill Deke. He was just the clean-up man.

Scooby Doo was offered up as the state's next witness. Deke's own mother had taken Scooby Doo in as a homeless child and raised him. Deke treated Scooby Doo like his younger brother.

Gilligan played for the jury Scooby's videotaped statement to Det. Rodriquez. During Scooby's interview, Rodriquez himself called Scooby a goddamn liar and told him he was tired of fucking with him. Scooby went on to admit that he was a liar and that basically he couldn't help it.

I asked Scooby all the questions I could think of to see what motivated him to do this to a member of his family. To this, the only truthful thing Scooby said was that after he got caught up, he could either be killed by Deke's people or by C-Bo's folks. This was funny because they were all related, except for Big-T, Hootie, and Bullet Proof. Scooby said his chances of living were better on C-Bo's team.

I asked Scooby if he could hear Deke flumping around in the trunk of the car. I asked him if he could hear Deke's head banging against the inside hood of the trunk and if he heard the inside trunk light burst, as Deke repeatedly struck it with his head. Did he hear Deke grasping for air and pleading for his life? Did he care about any of this, as Deke, his own brother, laid duct-taped in the trunk of Fabu's car?

I wanted to know how it smelled when they opened the trunk of the car; if Deke's shit and piss was too overbearing for him after he released himself. Deke had been in the trunk of one car or another for over eight hours. K.B. lined Fabu's trunk with plastic to avoid any of Deke's blood or fibers from being left behind.

I wanted Scooby to remember how they would periodically take him out of the truck or trunk and torture him. Did he participate in Deke's torture or did he just party and smoke weed with the others as they grew tired of beating Deke's ass?

I wanted Scooby to tell the jury if he remembered how cold it was that fall morning. If Scooby remembered how it rained all day. How dark it must have been for Deke in Fabu's trunk with a garbage bag over his head. Scooby knew Deke must have been cold and scared, as he was dying in that dark, damp trunk grasping for air, butt-ass naked.

When they did open the trunk, could Scooby see the bag as it expanded with Deke's every breath? Did Scooby hear Deke tell K.B. to "just go ahead and kill me, I'm tired?" Did Scooby hear Deke deny knowing where any cocaine was? Did Scooby say anything when K.B. told Deke to just wait for C-Bo? What was the look on Scooby's face when the bag over Deke's head stopped moving, when Deke eventually suffocated? I wondered if Scooby just smoked another blunt. I believed that Deke was dead after they removed him from the trunk of Fabu's car. I figured that C-Bo was evil, but not evil enough to dismember Deke while he was still alive.

I asked Scooby if he would just share with us what really went through his mind when they decapitated Deke's head and gave him his brother's head to bury. I thought Scooby could perhaps make some sense out of this evil and twisted shit to the jury.

He couldn't.

I positioned myself, as I questioned Scooby, to see if he had the nerves now to look at Deke's mother and wife here in the courtroom. This is the same family that took him off the streets; that fed and gave him a place to sleep. This was Deke's family. And it was his family. Without giving an answer, Scooby just squirmed and fidgeted like the rat he was.

Practicing all of this shit beforehand in my bathroom mirror appeared to be working.

After that, I decided to help Big-T, if I could, in my future examinations of all the witnesses. I was able to get most of them to admit that they didn't see Big-T and Hootie. At least for Big-T, all that was left were the testimonies of the concerned citizen and the newspaperman.

The rest was for Gilligan to work out and explain to the jury particularly, why K.B. torched Big-T's SUV. Gilligan then argued to the jury that C-Bo had a set of keys to Big-T's truck all the time. C-Bo just used the truck while Big-T was in Nashville for Thanksgiving. Perhaps, Big-T was in Nashville when most of this shit went down anyway.

Gilligan even challenged the jury to ask Det. Rodriquez why Doughboy had never been questioned. He was identified at Ying-Yang's house when Deke was first kidnapped. Besides, he had motive. It was Doughboy and C-Bo's coke. Afterwards, Gilligan showed the jury a picture of Doughboy. The resemblance of he and Big-T was striking. They could be twins. Both had fair complexions, bald heads, scruffy facial hair, and weighed over 300 pounds. Seemingly, Gilligan had somehow placed himself first and one, on the one-yard line, with Fabu's and closing arguments left.

Fabu admitted that as a condition of his release, he was to provide information on C-Bo and testify truthfully. As of the date of trial, Fabu had not provided the state with any information on C-Bo. At trial, Fabu came off like he thought he was — truly Fabulous and better than Big-T, Hootie, and Bullet Proof. Fabu strolled up to the witness stand wearing these beautiful shoulder length dreads, designer suit, and Payless shoes.

I had seen him in the same suit three times on three occasions. This was only a two-week trial. On the day Fabu received his probation, I told him Merry Christmas. Shit, maybe it was his lucky suit.

I looked at the Professor as this motherfucker had the unmitigated gall to say in open court that he was not like the others and that's why C-Bo trusted him. I asked him if C- Bo loved and trusted him like a brother. He said yes, as if he was saying to me, motherfucker ain't that what I just said. I asked Fabu, given C-Bo's love and trust of you, if he volunteered to set C-Bo up for arrest.

Fabu replied, "Yes." I asked, "if you would lie to your childhood friend who trusted and loved you, would you tell us anything?" Fabu then leaned back in his chair and crossed his legs. He cleared his throat and then told us that his answer depended on how his schizophrenia was acting on any given day. To the jury it didn't matter if Fabu was a cleanup-man or not. It was clear to them that he was just as responsible for Deke's death as C-Bo.

The state rested. The Professor went to work. The Professor lectured the jury for about an hour on why these defendants should not be found guilty. The Professor argued that whoever was present when K.B. returned with the chainsaw was guilty of Deke's murder. The Professor, using the medical examiner as proof, explained why Deke suffocated in the trunk. After the Professor sat down, there was nothing else to say. The jury deliberated for about three days.

Hootie was found not guilty of all charges. Big-T was found not guilty of all charges with the exception of kidnapping. The jury hung on that count 11-to-1 for conviction. Bullet Proof was found not guilty of murder, but guilty of concealing a homicide.

After the verdict was read, Bullet Proof hugged the Professor. Seeing a smile on Bullet Proof's face was a profound moment. It was funny to watch the Professor meticulously straighten up his suit afterwards. Apparently, the jury accepted Maple's testimony, as they did not believe K.B. Maple had identified Bullet Proof as one of the guys that helped put her old freezer on the U-Haul truck.

The District Attorney vowed to retry Big-T on the kidnapping charge. Eventually, Big-T made bond on that charge and was released from jail. To date, he has not been retried. I never heard from Hootie again, not even a thank you. I'm not surprised, that's just how niggas are. Hootie and Big-T's mother died before the trial started.

Seemingly, along with C-Bo, K.B, Fabu, and Scooby Doo, the three guys the state had let go were Deke's murderers. The boys from Nashville and Bullet Proof were outsiders and were supposed to be the fall guys, but that plan backfired.

Word has it that C-Bo was recently stopped by police. He was on a motorcycle and dressed in drag. Police mistakenly let him go. He has not been seen since. I still laugh to myself when I think about these dudes driving around in a U-Haul truck with a herby kirby containing body parts trying to buy some weed.

I guess that time will move on just as patience persists for justice for Deke. Sometimes, I think that Deke's life just caught up with him. I'm left numb when I think of how these dudes spent three days with Deke before they killed him. They were so patient and evil. The scariest thing is that the medical examiner said he didn't know if Deke was dead or alive before they cut him up. To imagine the unimaginable, Deke could have been hearing the chainsaw and feeling its blade as it severed his arm. That is, if they cut his arm off first. Unlike Abraham, after Deke's three-day journey to death, there was no ram in the bush.

I won't forget what Big-T's mother said to me, "Excuse me sir, but I didn't raise niggas that could do something like that to someone." I don't know if she did or not. C-Bo's mother apparently did. At the end of the day, Deke was dead and there was a trial where no one was found guilty of his murder. They just all helped clean up afterwards.

Sentence: Bullet Proof 10 years for concealing a homicide.

Chapter 4

Addiction

MOSES

He led many to the promised land, but he went too far.

On August 11, 2006, I stood in the pulpit and I told the mourners about the time I first met Moses. It had to be the summer of 1995. I told them how Moses was walking around the office with a picture of Betty telling everyone that this was his girl and he was going to marry her. At the time, Moses was one of the clerks at the Public Defender's Office and I was an assistant public defender. Moses was a third-year law student hired over the summer. I don't know if he was a paid clerk or was just around as a volunteer to get some trial experience. So as Moses made his way around the office, I guess it was obvious to him that I did my best to ignore him. Sensing my lack of interest, Moses placed a picture of his fiancé in my face and told me the bit, "This is my girl Betty and I'm going to marry her."

As a courtesy more so than genuine interest, I looked at the photo of Betty. I told the mourners how beautiful Betty was with the LPH (long pretty hair) and the beautiful brown complexion. Betty sported a smile that was sensual but revealing, with a touch of innocence. I could see why Moses thought he had a catch. But I was in no mood for celebrating marriage because at the time I was about to divorce my wife. So after I looked at Betty's photo, I told Moses that he wasn't ready for marriage.

Moses had a perplexed look on his face because up until now, we had never had a conversation. I did not know him nor did I know Betty or anything about their relationship or their respective families so, out of curiosity, Moses asked me why I thought that he was not ready for marriage. I told him that he first needed to graduate from law school, pass the bar exam, get a job, make a lot of money, lose it and make it again. Then, maybe Betty would marry him. As Moses removed Betty's picture from the table and placed it in his shirt pocket, Moses told me that he would indeed graduate from law school, then pass the bar exam, make a lot of money and afterwards, he and Betty would spend it together. Moses reminded me that everyone was not as selfish as me. Having married right out of law school, I felt like I had robbed myself of enjoying my professional life and all the perks and pussy that came with that.

I told the mourners how Moses added color to my life. That his personality had substance and texture, it was tangible, it was something you could feel or touch. To my resentment, Moses would call me Teddy. I told Moses that he had never met Teddy and he knew nothing about him. I told the mourners how Moses told me that he did not like Ted and to not bring him around him. Ted the Lawyer Man was too serious and self-conscious. Ted was the guy who lived on the edge of a cliff in a box. Moses told me that he called me Teddy because that's what my mother called me. Teddy, Teddy Bear, and finally he settled on Teddy Ball Game. Teddy Ball Game because I was always ready to fight somebody. Moses knew my stock. He knew where I was from in the world. Moses had an old soul.

At any rate, I found myself avoiding Moses. But a mutual friend, Walter, would oftentimes invite us to lunch. Walter had already shared with the mourners how Moses, myself and he would on occasion go to breakfast, leave breakfast and go over to Sylvia's for lunch, leave Sylvia's and have dinner at Houston's or Cheese Cake Factory or some other restaurant. But Sylvia's was our place. The waitresses and waiters loved us because we left big tips. They knew to bring Walter the corner ends in our cornbread basket and kept Walter and I filled up on Arnold Palmers. Moses was having either a Corona and lime or a Hennessy. It didn't matter to Moses that at times it was 11 a.m. in the morning.

I avoided Moses because I did not like his gratuitous use of the noun Nigga. I told Walter that Moses used the word Nigga as an adjective. If Moses liked you, he'd referred to you as "my Nigga." If he didn't like you, he would refer to you as a "bitch ass Nigga." If he was lukewarm toward you, he would refer to you as a "soft" or "lame Nigga." After I told Walter about my concerns with Moses, Walter told me "Nigga please," get in the truck and we went to Sylvia's.

I then looked to this sad audience and I saw people laughing and reflecting on their experiences with Moses. I reminded the mourners that it took a village to raise a child. I acknowledged Moses' parents and assured them that Moses had run the good race. As evidence of that, I asked the mothers of his Pee Wee football team to stand; then the mothers and kids of his Pee Wee baseball team; then the politicians, judges, and lawyers from various counties to stand. At the end, everyone in the church was standing. I asked them to look around at each other. Seemingly, Moses had been a community of one too many.

After the funeral, Walter and I reminisced about how he and Moses argued about Jesus. Walter's mother was an evangelist and he went on to major in religion in college. So Walter loved to bait people into philosophical arguments about the racial identity of Jesus. Moses was ready to fight Walter because Walter told Moses that he was in love with the Euro concept of Jesus. Walter ridiculed the picture of the white Jesus Moses' mother kept on the wall next to Martin Luther King, Jr. and John F. Kennedy. Moses, finding this offensive, challenged Walter to a fight. We were walking down Marietta Street when Moses professed his love for Jesus at the top of his lungs and began bumping his chest against Walter's. Moses wanted to fight right there and then but Walter's purpose was only to agitate Moses.

At the time, Moses weighed only 180 pounds. Walter was an ex-professional football player who was an easy 280 pounds and all muscle. For me, it was only the second time I had witnessed a man profess his love for God. The first time was when my cousin Cleve, a violent drunk, asked Frank, a family friend, who was a born again Christian, would he suck Jesus' dick to prove his love to Jesus. Frank said that he would. I recalled how my brother and his friends looked at Frank like he was a fag. The last time I saw my cousin Cleve alive was when I was driving on the west side of Indianapolis. I saw Cleve sleeping in a doorway. It was winter time. I regret that I kept driving. I know if Cleve had seen me sleeping in a doorway in winter, he would have taken me home. I knew that Cleve loved me, but I couldn't take it when Cleve would beat up my mother's sister and my uncle in his drunken rages. So I left him there on the street.

Walter then told me about how Moses accused this trick of killing a crackhead. Walter and Moses were representing Bonzo, a bisexual pimp. Bonzo was accused of killing a white boy who allowed Bonzo to fuck him in exchange for drugs. The white boy would then buy pussy from Bonzo's whores. Well, somehow, it got out that the white boy had Aids. So Bonzo killed him and the whores fled to Las Vegas. Moses made much of the fact that the whores were just as shitty as Bonzo, having learned that the white boy had Aids. Thus, they had motive and opportunity to kill the white boy too.

Moses asked the whore, "So you were there when the white boy was killed?" The Trick answered, "Yes." Moses: "So the white boy may have given you Aids?" The Trick answered yes again. And finally Moses asked the Trick, "You never called police from Las Vegas to report a murder?" The Trick replied she had not called police. Moses then said, "Because you didn't want to tell on yourself."

At the recess, the whore called Moses a black motherfucker and goddamn nigga liar as she walked into the women's restroom outside the courtroom. Walter told me that Moses asked the whore, "Who you calling a Nigga?" And the whore said, "I'm calling your trick ass a Nigga." As if Moses agreed that he was a motherfucker and a liar but he was not a nigga! Every time Walter tells me this story, I laugh until I cry. I can see Moses taking his time with each question wearing a suit that was too big for him, alligator shoes shinning. Seems like all of Moses' suits were too big and the sleeves fell to the end of his hands, where you could just see the tip of his fingers.

It was about midnight when Walter was outside of my house screaming my name. He told me that Moses was in the hospital around the corner from my house. Walter screamed that we needed to go see about him. I threw on my sweats and we were there within minutes. At the hospital, I met Moses' father for the first time. I had met his mother because she had worked as Moses' secretary. Moses' office was down the hall from mine on the sixth floor of the Maple Building. Moses' mother was a simple lady. She was well-versed in the Bible, but she told me that she was more spiritual than religious. She reminded me that it was folks from the church who had Jesus killed.

In the days before his death, Moses was being kept alive on a respirator. They say a prostitute ran into a restaurant and had them to call police. Moses had passed out behind the wheel of his truck. We learned that Moses was not only buying pussy, but he was self-medicating on crack cocaine.

I knew that Moses was having financial problems. He was divorcing his wife and was a single parent. Before they split up, apparently, Moses was even getting high with his wife. Thereafter, she started getting high and fucking a dude on the job. Moses, sad to say, had broken a sacred rule; never turn your wife on to drugs or lesbian relationships. She might just like it and start partying without you. They say that they found Moses' estranged wife in a crack motel. I heard the room was dark; infested with used crack sacks and dirty sheets. She was there with some dude that was getting her high and fucking her.

I regret that Moses stopped dating Neera, the lady of Indian descent. Moses really loved her as much as she loved him. Moses was dating and living with Neera when he went home for a visit with his daughters. While Moses was there, he fucked Betty. Betty got pregnant with Moses' son. Moses struggled over the decision to stay with Neera or return home to his pregnant wife. Neera asked Moses to stay. She would even adopt his kids. But Moses went back to Betty anyway.

At that time, I too was dating a lady of Indian descent, Shakura. Shakura and Neera were friends. Even though we all knew each other and had worked together at one time, Moses and I never socialized together with the Indian ladies. By the time Moses' son was four years old, both Neera and Shakura had married other men.

It's astonishing how a person can be a part of your life and you just don't know what they are going through. My friend was going through so much life that his brain exploded. The crack increased his blood pressure causing a vessel in his brain to burst. As he laid on that respirator for days, we fought over what would happen to his kids. At the time, Betty was in no position to care for them and Moses' parents had no parental rights as grandparents. I tried to be there for Moses' parents. His mother told me that I was her ram in the bush. At the time, I didn't know what that meant but as I sit here today, I'm still looking for my ram in the bush.

Sylvia's has since closed down but Walter and I still hop from one restaurant to the next. It's funny, because Walter didn't drink when Moses was alive. But now, Walter will order a Corona and a lime before we eat. I heard that Betty has cleaned herself up and the kids are okay. Betty even takes care of Moses' mother on a day-to-day basis. Moses' mom had become ill in recent years. Before she became ill, sometimes I would find her sitting on my front porch when I'd come home from work. She'd tell me that she didn't want anything but I knew I reminded her of Moses.

Moses is survived by two daughters and a son.

WRAPPED IN CELLOPHANE

Chocolate said that she wasn't running no goddamn where because she had nothing to do with this shit. As the car drove by the first time, they heard four or five shots. When the first shots rang out, everyone who was on the porch with Chocolate took cover, but Chocolate just stood there.

The car went up the street about a half of block and turned around. The occupants of the car switched seats before they returned, blasting off another four or five shots. When they came back the second time, Chocolate just stood there talking about she was celebrating her birthday as bullets flew all around her. Chocolate just stood there saying that she wasn't going to run no goddamn place 'cause she didn't do shit.

As Chocolate stood there, she was struck in the chest. Chocolate looked at Junior and told him she had been hit. I thought this was odd, because her boyfriend Dick was in the same area and she didn't tell him. But then, I thought, Chocolate was never really committed to one man.

After Chocolate told Junior she was hit, she took off running with her Colt 45 in hand toward the door. Chocolate managed to open the door and get inside. Junior lived in a shotgun house, much like the one I grew up in. As you entered the front door, there was a long hallway where one could enter into the various rooms. Like most shotgun houses, the kitchen was usually in the back of the house. Chocolate made it about five steps into the hallway of the house before she collapsed, her Colt 45 leaving her hand as she hit the floor. Thus, Chocolate did not fumble her Colt 45; she was down by contact when she hit the floor.

I thought that Chocolate's ability to hold on to her Colt 45 even though she'd been shot in the chest would make a great commercial for Colt 45 Malt Liquor. Then I thought about the extent of Chocolate's addiction. The shot pierced her heart with the bullet going through her chest and exiting through her back. And, still, Chocolate held on to her beer to the bitter end — addiction.

I've heard of people who are just tired of living and fighting with their addiction. In their depression, they have become tired of who they've become and tired of all the people that they've hurt. They've become tired of the failed hope that they have given those that loved them and the faith-based hope that they might one day beat this addiction. Regretfully, they have become tired of all the pussy that they have given away over the years. And to those of you who thought that you could outrun, outlast or outwit her addiction, she really did love you. Inevitably, her addiction was much more than they could understand. It was even more than she could understand.

The addict gets to a point where she just wants it to end. They have given up hope, the hope that we have for them, the last vestige of love. In this desire to end it all, they take chances that they would not normally take. They do stupid shit, like unprotected sex and not duck for cover when being fired upon. They take hold to the morbid reality that they through addiction have created for themselves. Sadly, their behavior becomes one of vicarious suicide.

I don't think anyone could tell us if Chocolate was tired of living or if she truly wanted to be shot. All they could tell us is that Chocolate didn't grab her chest when she was shot, she held on to her beer. That she didn't duck for cover as the shots rang out, she just stood there when everybody else ran. I can only surmise that Chocolate was tired of living. She was tired of boyfriends that she'd refuse to tell her real name and she was tired of random fucking. She missed her kids, but knew that they could never see her as she was. Chocolate knew through her addiction that she was wrapped in cellophane. Chocolate's addiction resulted in her vicarious suicide.

Clear, plastic cellophane can seal containers and keep food fresh. Cellophane is so transparent and clear one can see right through it. Cellophane is typically used to wrap up objects. Cellophane can also be used for restraint, control, and limitation. Its purpose is to secure the object from nicks, scrapes, scratches, and ultimately from being broken. However, when used incorrectly, such as for a baby crib liner, cellophane can cause death. Eventually, the baby dies a crib death as she suffocates from cellophane used to simply keep her mattress urine-free. When wrapped in cellophane, you can't breathe.

Sissy and Jesse Williams, brother and sister, and their cousin Melvin Clark were all on trial for Chocolate's murder. Melvin and Sissy were kissing cousins. The story goes that Melvin became upset with Sissy's ex-lover Junior, when Junior gave Sissy $100 and a baby gorilla as child support for his child. Junior was again successful in making Sissy look like a fool in front of everybody. This time Melvin got so upset that he decided to kill Junior.

Melvin and Sissy had been in a relationship for months after Sissy moved back to the old neighborhood. Melvin would buy her gifts, sundries, and perfume. They couldn't keep their hands off each other unless Melvin's wife was around, which was rare. Junior was jealous.

When Sissy was about 14 or 15 years old, she was living with the 24 or 25-year-old Junior. To say that Junior was a child molester would be too flattering of a description of him. Sissy told me how

Junior would rape and beat her as a teen. How he'd beat her when he had cocaine to snort and smoke, and beat her when he ran out. On one occasion, Sissy told me how Junior took her shoes and put her out in the rain, when he wanted to get high. Sissy had refused to leave their apartment and Junior didn't like to get high around her.

Sissy had no adult protection and she had no contact with her father. He left when she was a child. She told me that her mother was an absentee parent and an alcoholic. Sissy pretty much cooked and cleaned for her brothers, David, Jesse, and Marley. During the time that Sissy was with Junior, her brothers were too young and afraid to confront Junior. So Sissy's abuse went on for years until the family moved across town after Junior had gone to prison. Junior was sentenced to prison for cocaine and burglary charges.

By this time, however, Sissy was possibly pregnant with Junior's child. When Junior learned Sissy was pregnant, Junior believed that the child wasn't his, so Junior used every opportunity to argue with Sissy over child support. Junior would call his alleged son ugly and that the boy favored a baby gorilla.

Sissy never sought child support from the authorities against Junior. Just the same, Junior was afraid to go through the paternity process. Instead, Junior would just fuck with Sissy every time he saw her. By the time we went to trial for Chocolate's murder, Sissy was 28 years old and a high school dropout with four kids by different men.

On the day of the shooting, Sissy, Melvin, and Sara, her brother Jesse's girlfriend, were all hanging out at Sara's grandmother's house. Sara's mother was also home when Junior and his posse came over. Junior and Sara are cousins.

Junior would always surround himself with crackheads that he used as flunkies. On this day, Junior had Dick, his chauffeur, Craig and Patrice, Junior's new girlfriend as passengers as they drove over to Sara's house. When they walked into the house, Junior, Dick, and Craig all had guns in the waistbands of their pants. When Junior saw Melvin all hugged up with Sissy, Junior was jealous. So, Junior started talking shit about his alleged son that looked like a baby gorilla. Everybody who was in the room started laughing at Sissy, particularly Junior's posse.

Melvin then snatched Junior up by the collar; stuck a gun to his side and marched Junior out of the house. When everyone got outside, Junior and Melvin drew guns on each other. Dick and Craig ran for the car; Patrice took cover behind a tree. Sissy had followed them out of the house along with everyone else. Sissy then stood between Melvin and Junior pleading with them to put the guns down. Sara called police.

When the police arrived, it was Officer Lunch, the neighborhood beat officer, that gave a fuck. Everyone out there that day knew Lunch and couldn't stand him. Lunch was of average height, muscular build, and bald. He was an abuser. Lunch's reputation was that if he got out of his car, someone got his or her ass kicked. If he had to write a report, someone got arrested. As Officer Lunch was pulling up, Junior was pulling off in his car with his crew. Melvin was standing next to the open trunk of his car presumably putting up his gun.

Lunch slowly rode through traveling about 5 miles an hour, if that, looking at everybody's face and everybody was looking at him. Seemingly, Lunch looked at them niggas and just kept going. Lunch didn't even stop to investigate or make a report of the "shots fired" call Sara had placed to 911. At trial, when we asked him why, he told us that he tries to do as little as possible because he does not like to come to court and testify. To me, Lunch had just confessed to us that he was a ghetto cop.

A ghetto cop is a police officer who over the years has become numb to all the crime that occurs in the ghetto. He has become apathetic to the ignorance and bullshit of its people. Like most of us, the officer has forgotten about all of the good people who are just stuck in the ghetto because they can't afford to live anywhere else. To that extent, the officer takes on the hopelessness attitudes of the people he has sworn to protect. He has become so worn down with the people and random violence in the community that he becomes a ghetto cop.

Had Lunch investigated, both Melvin and Junior would have been arrested. Thus, Chocolate could have still been alive to officially celebrate her birthday that was just two days away. After Lunch rode through, Melvin hooked up with Jesse. Melvin and Sissy had encountered Jesse, Marley, and Lydia, another one of Jesse's girlfriends, a few blocks from Sara's house. Melvin then explained to Jesse what had occurred between him and Junior. Melvin then got into Jesse's car with Marley and Lydia. Lydia then got into Melvin's car with Sissy and she drove Lydia home.

Melvin, Jesse, and Marley then drove across town to swap guns with Melvin's cousin. After they swapped guns, Melvin, Jesse, and Marley did a drive-by shooting on Junior. Intending to shoot Junior, Chocolate was shot through the left side of her chest.

Junior, Patrice, Craig, and Dick, Chocolate's boyfriend, were all present when Chocolate was shot. The shooting occurred just as night was falling. Before the shooting, Junior told police that he and the guys were drinking beer and corn liquor, white lighting. Chocolate had crack cocaine in her system; however, no one admitted to getting high with her.

As Chocolate's so-called-boyfriend Dick testified, it was obvious that I despised Dick as much as he despised me. He hated me for what I was and what he was not. He found me to be a sellout to the white man's way of life. I knew, however, that I had obtained something that Dick would have for himself, if he could. Dick was tall and dark but on the other side of handsome. His constant crack use had caused his teeth to fall out and his hair was cut short but nappy. Dick was street smart, but had no street credibility because he was a crackhead.

Although in his forties, the only thing that Dick had ever done for as long as he's smoked crack was shit, eat, and breathe. The hate Dick had for me was something tangible. One could feel the angst between us and I was the mirror of which we saw each other. It was as if we had not looked at ourselves in such a long time and when we did, we could see the deficiencies in each other.

Dick viewed me as an educated fool, a square trying to talk white, overly compensating to my white colleagues to fit in and get along. To him, I was as corny as any white boy not deserving of wearing my dark black skin. To Dick, I wasn't a black man, I just had black skin; I was an Uncle Tom, a sellout. This was so because to him, I did not empathize with his struggle of addiction, lack of education, opportunities, and wealth.

To Dick, I was wrapped in cellophane, living a life that was only measured by the white man's perception of success and his glass ceiling. Just like every other nigga that made it, eventually I would be suffocated and killed because I didn't pay my taxes. However, there was no way for Dick to know about my brother who died from a drug overdose in 1985 or my other brother's cocaine-induced heart attack in 1987. Dick didn't know me at all and what I've gone through to be me.

To me, Dick was the antithesis of what people had died and struggled for, to educate their children, to enjoy the right to vote, to live as free men and women. Dick had thrown all this away. In exchange, Dick just wanted to suck on a glass or metal pipe used to smoke crack cocaine.

Here we are again, two black men accusing each other of self-hatred. Here we are again, two black men standing on opposite sides of the street. So it goes, put two niggas together and they can't agree on anything. They can't even agree to disagree because they don't trust each other enough. Is it something in our DNA or just learned behavior like Willie Lynch said? Willie Lynch could not have known us so well.

Dick testified, as all crackheads do, that he saw and knew everything. When Dick was shown a picture that there were two poplar trees in the front yard where the shooting occurred and not just one as he testified, Dick accused the lawyer of having recently planted the tree to trick him. However, the trees were at least 100 years old.

Dick said he was Chocolate's boyfriend, but he didn't know her birth name. Suddenly, our trial had become Dick's minstrel show.

My hesitant and uncomfortable laughter as Dick testified was one of shame. Through Dick's crackhead shuffle and fidgetiness, the minstrel show went on for our white jurors and lawyers. However, our judge, prosecutor, and court reporter were recently divorced black females. I thought to myself after this, that they would never marry another black man.

My colleagues were an Irish female for Jesse and a Jewish male for Melvin. There were three black jurors, two black females, and a retired male schoolteacher who looked rather grandfatherly. As Dick continued to testify, I and the grandfather made eye contact. Thereafter, like me, I noticed that the retired teacher began to wear his shame as well.

Craig had fallen asleep at the homicide office before they could take his statement regarding Chocolate's murder. When he woke up, Craig refused to speak with the police because he was too tired, so he says. Craig told us that he was about 40 years old. He told us that he has been hearing voices inside his head since 1969. Craig was a chubby dude with a brown complexion that sported a bald, shaved head. Homeless, Craig was an admitted crackhead. By just looking at Craig, with his eyes rolling back in his head and his slow speech, you could tell that he was certifiably crazy but too dumb to lie. Less than four years ago, Craig was arrested when police caught him walking down the street with a television set in his hands.

Upon closer inspection, the television was the property of the elementary school across the street from the cat hole where he lived. Again, the jury laughed at the idea of Craig walking down the street with a television set in his hand. Craig was rather flippant as he explained to the jury that he had bought the television set from another crackhead because he could get a better price. The fact that the television belonged to the school children never crossed his mind. Craig did two years in prison for stealing the television set.

Craig, Dick, and Chocolate all stayed in the same abandoned

house they called a cat hole, next door to Junior. Both Junior's home and the cat hole were across the street from the elementary school and the church parking lot.

As we cross-examined Craig, with all the psychotropic drugs he had taken because of the voices, one truly didn't know if one was questioning Craig or having a debate with the voices inside of his head. As I sat there listening to Craig go back and forth on what he remembered or had forgotten, I noticed that Craig was wearing a throwback sports jersey, dingy blue jeans and some dirty old gym shoes.

I was always taught that you dress for court like you're going to church. I thought to myself, either people just don't care about any of our sacred institutions anymore or they are just too poor to care. I then reminded myself that a crackhead doesn't respect anyone or anything; just the one who's holding the crack. The crackhead's moral compass is broken much like the entertainer who will show the world her naked-ass pussy or do or say anything to be seen, get a laugh, or seek approval.

Junior was supposed to be dead but instead, Chocolate took his bullet. Junior's bullshit got Chocolate killed. Everybody who knew Junior — friends and family — said that Junior loved to start shit. Junior always wanted to be the big man, that's why he kept crackheads and drunks around him. Junior would use them as flunkies. Dick was his chauffeur and Craig was his 'do boy' for odd jobs and such. By the time we made it to trial, Junior had married Patrice and she was a drunk.

Before Junior testified, I told my white female colleague to tear into Junior's ass. I wanted her to drill his ass for giving Sissy $100 and a baby gorilla for child support. I figured this type of examination coming from another woman, a mom, would be potent enough to bring Junior the shame and lack of character we needed to show the jury. To the contrary, she told me that it would be difficult to get Junior to disrespect her because she was a white woman. But he would challenge me because I was another black man.

It hurts me to know that white folks aren't blind to the slave ways of the "so called" modern African-American. My white colleagues know that black folks respond differently to them than they do to their own. This is so, even if we have more money, education, and experience than our white colleagues. Sadly, there is a yes'suh master and no'suh master mentality that still exists. As much as I try to forget this cultural fact, I see it every day and not just here in the South.

My oldest brother died just a few weeks ago. He was 67 years old. I referred my sister-in-law to two medical malpractice attorneys that routinely win million dollar verdicts. My sister-in-law asked me whether the attorneys were black. Seemingly, it didn't matter to her as much whether they were successful or not. She was concerned about their race. My sister-in-law is from Harlem, N.Y.

The white female attorney was right. As she asked Junior questions, he answered with a series of "yes'suh" and "no'suh" responses. I was embarrassed by Junior's blackness. Sometimes as an educated black man, you can't separate your blackness from those that look just like you. That "you're only as strong as your weakest link mentality" was ingrained in me as a child. For me, this attitude has exceeded the boundary of just family. It has poured into the vast community of all black people, a vastness I cannot control and is beyond my comprehension. Thus, I keep reminding myself that I can only speak for myself.

Today, I was ashamed that Junior couldn't express himself like a 40-year-old man. Rather, this man spoke with great difficulty and a heavy tongue; like a slave. I thought to myself, how do I rationalize the respect I have for the slaves who sacrificed and toiled for me and on the other hand, despise my brother, who sounds like one?

I don't recall in my own ignorance if I ever sounded or articulated as poorly as Junior articulated. However, I do know that my sisters would not have stood for it. See, my sisters realized that I was their representative when I left the house and they understood that my diction was evidence of their ignorance. Also, in my neighborhood, it was something to be called a Mississippi nigga. Although, we were from Mississippi so was everyone else in the neighborhood. Like most people from the South, my sisters and brothers wanted to be citified. Being called a Mississippi nigga was worse than being called a nigga. However, the former epithet was considered fighting words.

Just as it disappoints me that some African-Americans think to speak with proper grammar is an attempt to be white, it is just as offensive to me when some white folks offend the black community. They think that they can just run to Jesse or Al and apologize. Don't get me wrong, Al and Jesse are good people; they just don't represent the folks I know.

Junior denied the fact that he was a troublemaker and a shit starter. He asked me where I got my information. Summarily, I told him his cousins. Junior denied smoking crack around Sissy, but admitted that he was smoking when he dated her. Junior told the jury that he didn't beat Sissy and put her out in the rain with no shoes on. She had left on her own. I asked Junior to admit that he essentially likes fucking under-aged girls. To this, Junior said, Sissy was 17 years old when they got together. To all of my questions, it was clear to the jury that Junior was a liar.

I asked Junior if Sissy was in the car during the drive-by shooting. He said that he wasn't sure but it looked to be a woman riding in the back seat as the car drove by. As the shots rang out, I asked him if he recognized Sissy's voice coming from the car. He said no but it sounded like a woman. I asked if Marley, Sissy's younger brother, looked and sounded liked a woman. Junior said yes, that Marley looked and sounded like a big old girl. The jury laughed as Junior, in his coarse broken English, testified. Unbeknownst to Junior, Sara and Cathy had already described to the jury Marley's weight problem and the cheap perm that fell to his shoulders. At trial, none of the witnesses wanted to come out and say that Marley was a big old fag, but it was clear that that's what was intimated.

By this time, Junior, Craig, and Dick had all identified Jesse's car and they identified Melvin as the shooter. As shots rang out, they all claimed that they heard a woman yell from the car "you're going to take care of this goddamn baby." Craig never saw the back seat passenger, but believed it to have been a woman. Junior had previously told police that he saw Sissy in the back seat of the car. However, at trial, he admitted that he lied to police when he told them it was Sissy. I showed the jury that Junior was used to lying to police because on his arrest records. He had used five different aliases on five separate arrests.

To the contrary, Dick was the only one who stuck by his position that it was Sissy he observed in the back seat of Jesse's car. Dick swore that he didn't care how many trees we had planted to trick him. Patrice told the police and the jury that she didn't see anything. To everyone's confusion, Patrice started talking about who had fried the chicken when the shots were fired.

Marley took the witness stand with his cheap perm intact. He was only about 21 years old but he weighed nearly 300 pounds. There was nothing masculine about Marley that anyone could see; he was just this big feminine looking dude with these long fingernails professing his innocence. At trial, Marley would take a deep breath and say, "I wasn't in the car at the time of the shooting." Marley took another deep breath, and when he told the jury that after Chocolate was killed, Junior and his posse came by and shot up his mother's house.

The police were called out to the scene and shell casings were collected. Surprisingly, the casings recovered matched some of the casings recovered from Junior's house. To the dismay of the police, there was evidence of a shootout at Junior's place that was never investigated. The shell casings from the Marley shooting were given to police. The police acknowledged that they recovered the casing but the lead detective, a ghetto cop, lost them. For the defense, this was a major occurrence because it suggested a self-defense claim; a 'who fired first' type of theory. Did Junior fire first or was it Melvin?

Things were going well for the defense team until Jesse's

attorney made a tactical mistake. She had hired a private investigator (P.I.) to assist her in her preparation for the trial. Her P.I. had a wealth of experience at gathering information. As a witness, he even presented well in front of the jury. As he testified about distances and measurements, the only real significant testimony needed from him was the time the sun went down on the day of the shooting. Thus, was it dark outside at the time of the shooting or was there some daylight left. Jesse's attorney could have presented the newspaper for such information without calling the P.I. as a witness, but she didn't and this mistake proved fatal to Jesse's defense.

The District Attorney asked the P.I. if he had read Jesse's statement that he had given to police. Jesse's statement up until this point had been kept from the jury for technicality reasons. The rule is if Jesse didn't testify, then certain parts of his statement are kept from the jury. However, if Jesse did testify, the jury could hear his statement. The P.I. stated that he had, in fact, read Jesse's statement. The P.I. went on to tell the jury how Jesse told police that he drove the car as shots were fired from his car and Marley and not Sissy was in the backseat.

Now forced to testify in his own defense, Jesse tried to correct the mistake his lawyer had made. Jesse told the jury that he could not have been present for the shooting because he was out buying some stolen tires. Second mistake; never have a client confess to another crime as an alibi for the first crime. Jesse had initially told police he drove the car at Melvin's request because Melvin had threatened to kill him. Months prior to the shooting, he told police that he had tried to have Melvin arrested for pistol-whipping him. Jesse even had the police reports to prove it.

Jesse went on to tell police that when he encountered Melvin, Lydia did get into Melvin's car with Sissy. Melvin then got into Jesse's car with him and Marley. Furthermore, he and Melvin switched positions after the first rounds of shots. Melvin was the driver the second time around when Chocolate was hit. Thus, either Jesse lied to police about his statement or he was lying to the jury about the stolen tires.

Melvin took the witness stand and was dead set on not conceding anything. Melvin just started lying from the words "do you promise to tell the truth?" Melvin was married with two or three kids. His father and Sissy's grandfather were brothers. Melvin stood about 6'2," 230 pounds, muscular with slight facial hair in a goatee. He presented well as he testified, but his shit was so different from everybody else you knew somebody had to be lying.

Melvin would have been a lot more believable if he had just told the jury, "We were riding down Junior's street and he fired on us first before we fired back." There were no independent witnesses that could have contradicted Melvin's story.

Melvin's version could have been just as believable as Junior's posse; certainly with evidence of different shell casings being found in Junior's yard. But Melvin told the jury he wasn't there. Moreover, that Sara was mistaken when she said that he and Junior drew guns down on each other at MaDear's house. Melvin even denied that he had been in a romantic relationship with Sissy as jurors observed Sissy hit me on my leg in disbelief to Melvin's lie. Melvin claimed that Jesse lied because Jesse knew that Sara had come on to him and he rebuffed her. Junior was jealous of him because of his relationship with Sissy and Junior's posse lied about him because Junior told them to. Essentially, everybody lied about Melvin.

Lydia was supposed to have been Sissy's alibi witness. At the time of the shooting, Lydia was another one of Jesse's women. Lydia admitted to the jury that she knew that Jesse was still dating Sara but she didn't care. Jesse had told the jury that Lydia had gotten into Melvin's car with Sissy. Jesse also told us that Lydia had given him the money to buy the stolen tires. At trial, however, it was learned that Lydia was now dating and pregnant by Melvin's brother. Thus, the only way she could help Sissy was to incriminate Melvin.

I told the jury we had to track Lydia down and that she was not forthcoming in an attempt to help Melvin. I knew Lydia would suddenly have amnesia about everything and that she would Scooby Doo us with her "I don't know," but to see through her bullshit. Imagine the presence of mind or the misplaced priorities of love, when one would send another to prison for life and to lie in an effort to save the brother of her baby's daddy.

At the trial, over 20 people testified. However, no one really knew Chocolate's real name until the end. Certainly, her name was mentioned in the beginning but that's where it was lost, in the beginning. At the end of the trial, the prosecutor became upset when the Irish attorney refused to use Chocolate's birth name, Lisa Williams. The Irish attorney referred to her as Chocolate throughout the entire trial. For that, the Assistant District Attorney basically called her a racist. The Irish Attorney only called Chocolate what Chocolate called herself. I guess the prosecutor wanted her to show Lisa Williams some dignity in death.

As we progressed through this trial of self-hatred, addiction, ignorance, jealousy, stereotypes, and identity crisis, we learned that many of us are still trapped between the image we have of ourselves and the perception of others we try to live up to.

Seemingly, some of us are crippled by our inability to dream because of our inability to escape the splintered reality of our own addictions. More and more of our inner city communities become lost in the notion of community development and self-improvement. While in the same communities, the addicts sink lower and lower into addiction, and will now steal the television equipment used to teach our children.

Sadly, our communities die as transparent efforts of re-gentrification are born. Still, we are sucked into this vacuum of "I want to live on the other side of town, away from all of the bullshit," even if we have to drive two hours to work or school while our communities die from the cancer of addiction. The livable community becomes smaller and smaller but we do nothing, even though we see this slow death coming. Instead, we'd rather suffocate before we help each other. Why? Because as a society I think that we're just trapped in the wasteland of cellophane.

It was later learned that Junior was not in fact the father of Sissy's baby. However, I'd like to think that Lisa Williams didn't die in vain. At least, Lisa, a.k.a. Chocolate's murder trial forced everyone to look at themselves.

Sentence: Melvin Clark and Jesse Williams sentenced to life in prison plus 40 years.
Sissy Williams: Acquitted.

CHAIN REACTION

And there was light and the light was good.

Genesis 1:4

When Meatball saw Lil Momma's face, he rode his bike down the street yelling that Pretty Tony had beat up Lil Momma. Lil Momma was just sitting on the curb with her cane and Pretty Tony was standing over her in her space. When Lil Momma saw Meatball, she got up from the curb and began walking down the street crying.

As he rode his bike through the neighborhood, Meatball screamed as if there were a fire in a crowded theater; he screamed like he was 10 years old. Meatball, of course, was chubby and had a round face. He reminded me of myself when I was his age — food around my mouth, beaded hair and caked dirt on my elbows all the way down to my wrists. I, too, was into everybody's business. However, Meatball proved to be one of the best witnesses the state had. At least, he wasn't a drug dealer or user.

It all started when Pretty Tony had offered to smoke his hit of crack cocaine and share a shot of brown liquor with Lil Momma. When they smoked up half the rock and drank the little liquor, Pretty Tony left two dollars and a half-rock of crack with Lil

Momma. Pretty Tony didn't tell me why he left his stuff with a crackhead. He just said that he went to buy another shot of liquor. When Pretty Tony returned, the crack and the two dollars were gone. Lil Momma claimed that Pretty Tony had taken the half rock of crack with him and she didn't know what happen to the two dollars.

Believing that Lil Momma was trying to play him, Pretty Tony commenced to beat her ass. I asked him if he was forgetting something. At first, he told me that that was the story. I told him that I didn't believe him because something was missing. It was as if he knew what I was thinking without me saying anything. As I looked at him, he denied fucking her.

Pretty Tony told me that he beat Lil Momma like she was a dude. He would beat and punch Lil Momma in the face and then rest, before he'd start on her again. He repeated this process at least three times before he realized that he would have to kill Lil Momma, but she still wasn't going to give him back his two dollars and the half- rock of crack that she had stolen from him.

After Meatball had spread the news of Lil Momma's beating, it was as if the whole neighborhood began looking for Pretty Tony. By this time, Pretty Tony had attempted to escape by running over to Dinky's Momma's house. They were related by marriage. Pretty Tony tried to hide himself in one of the bedroom closets. He was small enough, only 5'7" and crackhead skinny; he weighed only 125 pounds. Pretty Tony was very dark and hadn't ever been to a dentist. His bucked teeth extended to his chin. I found him, however, to be reasonably articulate.

At least 20 people came over to Dinky's mother's house. There was Red, Mimi, Rocky, Blue, and the children. They banged on Dinky's door demanding to come in. Inside Dinky's house were his mother, younger sister and brother — they were both teenagers. Nuke also lived at Dinky's house, but he wasn't home. A few months prior, Nuke had just been released from prison after serving time for shooting someone.

Dinky's mother refused to open the door for the mob waiting outside. Eventually, Smoke showed up and began to try to reason with Dinky's mom but she still refused to open the door. Smoke told her he just wanted to talk to Pretty Tony to see what happened. But Dinky's mother still refused to open the door. Smoke and Mimi were an item. Lil Momma was Mimi's mother, so Smoke felt compelled to do something since his old lady was upset after hearing what Pretty Tony did to Lil Momma.

Smoke was about 6'4," 325 lbs. and was black as smoke. He didn't look so much like the athletic type as much as that of a trucker. However, it was obvious that Smoke could handle himself. After Dinky's mom refused to open the door for Smoke, he just kicked the door in. When the door opened, the whole neighborhood ran inside the house. Mimi said that they found Pretty Tony hiding in a bedroom closet. As Smoke dragged Pretty Tony's ass out of the closet, part of the mob of men, women, and children commenced to beat his ass. The other part of the mob ransacked Dinky's mom's house.

The mob beat Pretty Tony's ass until they got tired. Mimi told me that she tried to make Pretty Tony's eyes look like Lil Momma's. Do unto him as he had done to her mother. They tore the clothes off Pretty Tony's back. However, being as black as he was, his injuries were not as visible as Lil Momma's.

After the beating, Lil Momma had two black eyes and a swollen head. Some say that her head had gotten as big as a lion. Lil Momma only weighed 98 pounds soaking wet anyway. After he had spread the news, Meatball saw Lil Momma walking down the street with her walking cane crying like a lost child. I think the size of her swollen head is what really scared Meatball the most.

After putting that ass-whipping on Pretty Tony, the mob eventually left. They laughed and joked about how they tore the clothes off Pretty Tony's half-homeless ass. They rehashed how Smoke dragged him from the closet like a sack of dirty clothes. They laughed all the way back down to Tasha's house. Tasha lived right down the street about three good blocks, if that, from Dinky's momma's house. They sat on Tasha's huge Georgia porch and talked shit about Pretty Tony getting what he deserved for beating up a cripple.

While the raid was going on, Dinky's sister had called Dinky at his girlfriend's house. She told Dinky what happened. She described in her fear and hysteria how they beat Pretty Tony's ass and how they ransacked the house. Babysister also called Nuke and told him the same thing. Dinky and Nuke arranged to meet at John John's house in Decatur, a suburb of Atlanta. While there, John John gave Nuke a ghetto version of a modified 9 mm rifle with a handgun grip. It was certainly a weapon that had an identity crisis. One didn't know if it was a rifle or a handgun. Whatever it was, it proved fatal.

Nuke and John John got into Dinky's car and they drove over to Dinky's house. Pretty Tony was still breathing hard from the ass whipping he had gotten. They saw the condition of the house. Shit was strewn everywhere; there was broken furniture and glass, and papers. Nuke told them, "Let's ride." Dinky's mother tried to talk Dinky out of going. She tried to explain to Dinky that she was about to move to another neighborhood in a matter of weeks anyway. But Dinky could not let his boys ride without him; especially, when it was his mother who was violated. Nuke said, "Fuck them niggas." They could have gotten Pretty Tony any time, but they knew better than to come up in there.

Pretty Tony and John John got in to the backseat. Dinky was the driver and Nuke, with the ghetto gun, got in the front seat on the passenger side. They drove down to Tasha's house because they knew that's where everybody hung out. When they pulled up, there were people who participated in Pretty Tony' s beat down and there were people who were just there. Nuke just opened fire on the house. As the shots rang out, men, women, and children were running and ducking for their lives. Witnesses claimed that Pretty Tony was pointing people out for Nuke to shoot. As Nuke fired on the house, he was yelling out to them, "You motherfuckers know me! Every time I see one of you motherfuckers, I'm going to blast you!" Tasha was in the house asleep.

They say Nuke fired over ten rounds at the house and then they piled back into Dinky's car and drove back to his Momma's house. Hearing the gunfire, Tasha woke up and went outside. They told her what had happened to Lil Momma and what was done in revenge. They told her Nuke, Dinky, and Pretty Tony just did a drive-by with another dude and shot up the house. Tasha told them that she and Rocky had just smoked a blunt with Nuke yesterday on her porch to celebrate his release from prison. She thought that she and Nuke were cool. Tasha claimed that Nuke knew that those were her kids that were on the porch.

When Tasha decided to go talk to Nuke, everyone tried to talk her out of it, but she told them, "What's he gon' do, kill me?" Tasha, dressed in her pajamas, put her Nike's on and started walking down the street to Dinky's house. Rocky was with her. Either Pretty Tony or Dinky told Nuke that someone was coming. They could only tell that it was a chick and a dude. As they got closer, Nuke could tell that it was Tasha. Before she could say anything, Nuke shot Tasha in the face; she was dead on the scene. Tasha was only 25 years old. She left behind five kids and she was two weeks pregnant with child number six. Rocky fled.

Nuke, Dinky, John John, and Pretty Tony were all charged with Tasha's murder. John John made bond and fled. At trial, it was Nuke, Dinky, and Pretty Tony. Seemingly, Nuke was prepared to fall on the sword. Nuke told the jury that it was his gun that he kept at Dinky's house in his room. Nuke told the jury that no one encouraged him or directed him to shoot Tasha. He acted alone. I was okay with all of that since Nuke said nothing to hurt Pretty Tony or Dinky.

Pretty Tony told me he could not believe all of this shit was happening over a half-rock, two dollars, and some pussy. I told him I knew you had fucked her or you were shitty that she smoked your rock up and didn't fuck you the way you thought she ought to. He told me it went down something like that. But he did enjoy watching me defend him. Pretty Tony told me that I looked like I enjoyed this shit. I told him that we had different taste in what we enjoyed. I asked him how he could expect to enjoy fucking someone who walked with a cane. Pretty Tony laughed but I was serious.

During the trial, with a police escort, we loaded the jury onto a bus and took them to the scene where Tasha was killed. When we got there, I had one of the most surreal experiences of my life. I noticed that the makeshift cross that the neighbors had built was still standing in the place where Tasha was shot and died.

At the same time, school was letting out for the day. Standing on the corner of Elm Street and Simpson Road, there were so many prostitutes in tight revealing mini-skirts picking their babies up from the school bus. They sported an assortment of wigs — brunettes, platinum blonds, and red heads. The babies, in all of their innocence, were holding their mothers' hands. It was as beautiful as much as it was revealing of how momma' is just momma' in most life circumstances. I wondered which one of these kids would become the genius. I know that God likes playing those types of tricks on us.

When we returned to the courtroom, we thought that Nuke's acceptance of responsibility for everything would make everything go away. However, for some reason, Dinky's attorney, a former prosecutor, felt it was important that Dinky and Pretty Tony not get away with a lie. We all knew that Dinky was present when Nuke got the gun from John John, and that the gun was not kept in Nuke's room right before the shooting. Basically, Dinky's lawyer convinced Dinky's stupid ass to tell on himself and he did. Dinky told the jury everything about the gun including who was present during the shooting. Dinky told jurors that he was the driver of the car in the drive-by shooting. Even though no one could identify him as the driver, they just knew it was his car.

As the jury read their verdict and I was gathering up my case files, I imagined that at the end of the day, after everybody learned that Tasha had died, Lil Momma smoked that half rock she had stolen from Pretty Tony as she mourned Tasha's death. I guess she had two dollars on a dime hit if anybody was buying another one. So it was, Pretty Tony and Dinky were convicted of aggravated assault for their part in shooting up Tasha's house and were sentenced to 15 and 12 years to serve in prison, respectively.

Sentence: Nuke life in prison plus forty years.

NOT LIKE ME

When I received a call from a female colleague of mine, I was excited about picking up another murder case. I didn't care what type of murder case it was. To me, it was an opportunity to make some money. I've never been so wrong about a case. Domestic violence is a murder waiting to breathe its venom into the mouth of ordinary people. Yes, I'm convinced that anyone is capable of committing murder, especially if you've ever been married.

I thought that I would be able to identify with my client, Kenneth, since I too was going through a divorce. I understood how easily a woman could connive and manipulate in subtle but invidious ways. Being as angry as I was coming into the case, my opinion of black women wasn't very high. I believed that most black women were cowards who hid behind their pseudo femininity. So it goes without saying, I conveniently exploited or pushed my position to the extreme. This included fucking every woman who wanted to fuck me, and flirting with my wife's friends that I knew were open to the idea of fucking me. What a pathetic group friends.

So there I sat with Kenneth, a man of forty something years, B.S. in engineering and honorable military service. Kenneth was at one time a husband and a father. I don't know how many kids Kenneth had, but I knew that he had no contact with them. Kenneth was charged with murder. He was accused of beating his girlfriend in the head with a leg of a coffee table.

Kenneth was either so angry with women or so misogynistic that he hated the woman he had killed. The female attorney who referred his case to me, the female judge that presided over his case, and his own mother. The only female that Kenneth would tolerate was his sister, the lesbian. She was in the military and stationed in Arizona. Seemingly, Kenneth could only be represented by a man because of his profound dislike for women. But, quietly, no one knew I shared Kenneth's contempt.

When I met Kenneth, I soon learned that he was HIV positive. A long time drug user, Kenneth picked up his habit in the military. As I went over the facts of the case with him, it got more and more gruesome.

Kenneth had repeatedly bludgeoned the victim about the head with the leg of a coffee table. Kenneth had broken the table as he smashed it against the floor and then the wall, as the victim ran upstairs into the master bedroom. Kenneth and the victim shared a two-bedroom apartment. The victim attempted to close and lock their bedroom door, but Kenneth kicked the door in with his size 13 foot. He kicked so hard that he kicked the door out of its frame.

Kenneth stood as tall as me at about 6'3," and weighed over 200 pounds when I met him. The victim then ran and hid in the bedroom closet. I saw the pictures of her bloody palm prints inside the closet door. She was trying to keep him out. Kenneth told me that she pleaded with him to let her go. She told Kenneth that she was sorry, but Kenneth told me that he was tired of her shit. I kept asking Kenneth, "What did she do? What made you so angry?" He would only say that he got tired of her trying him.

At some point during one of my many interviews with Kenneth,

I felt the victim's anguish and fear as she ran from Kenneth. I heard her pleading with him because there was no one to call. See, Kenneth, during the attack, had ripped the phone cords from the wall to prevent her from calling 911. I could see her tears as they streamed down her face and mixed with her blood, begging Kenneth "Let me live. I'm sorry Kenneth," as Kenneth repeatedly bludgeoned her with the end of that table leg.

The crime scene pictures showed the trail of blood leading from the bedroom to the stairs and ultimately to the living room. Kenneth had dragged the victim's body from the upstairs bedroom to the living room. The stairs reflected how her head bounced like a basketball on each step as Kenneth dragged her by her legs downstairs. After dragging her downstairs, Kenneth finished the assault until she stopped moving. He then went next door and called police. Kenneth actually waited for the police to arrive. He then told police some bullshit about the victim breaking into his home and he killed her in self-defense. After going over these facts with Kenneth, I said to myself that Kenneth's contempt for the victim was complete.

After discussing all of these facts with Kenneth, he was still unflinching. His attitude was that the bitch deserved to die. I can only surmise that you can't ever steal and shoot up an addict's drugs and live to talk about it.

Kenneth never confessed to me, like most of my clients eventually do. He was steadfast in his attempt to control me like he was my superior officer and I was a mere private. Kenneth never asked me for shit. Everything was a directive.

As I began to look myself in the mirror, I needed to feel that I had nothing in common with Kenneth. As angry as I was with my wife and as vindictive as I tried to be, my weapon of choice was my dick. Hence, my emotional war could not have been as detrimental or destructive as Kenneth's physical war. Kenneth's war resulted in death.

My war resulted in my wife finding some new or different dick. I mean even if she did, I'm the one who left, right? I mean, if she did grieve for me to come back home, she wasn't going to grieve forever since she wasn't going to live forever. No way, I'm not like Kenneth. Kenneth was a military man, a Marine trained to kill. I, as a lawyer, was only trained to be persuasive; to manipulate facts if I'm good enough to get away with it. I'm aware of my inherent contradictions. I know nothing about killing people; only defending those who do. I could never be as complete in my training as Kenneth was with his. If I am, how do I live with my guilt? Kenneth had no guilt or mercy. So, I am different because I do. Yes, I do have mercy in my heart.

Kenneth was indeed my mirror and I couldn't bear to look at myself. Kenneth began to suffer from dementia and paranoia from his illness. However, in a lucid moment, he complained to the authorities that I failed to visit him. His complaint was justified. I admit that the mirror would not lie to me. When I did go to visit Kenneth, I informed him that I quit. He told me to go fuck myself. I told him I already had in fucking with him in the first place. Thereafter, as irony would have it, Kenneth was appointed an openly gay attorney for his trial. He was convicted of murder. Early into his sentence, Kenneth died from an Aids-related illness.

Sentence: Life in prison.

RIDDLE ME THIS

And he thought that we were friends. This attitude of friendship towards me was not uncommon from Riddle. See, a number of clients mistake my passion for winning as a likable quality associated with my favor for them. They want me to believe that the system has wronged them somehow; that they are the victims. My clients think that if I believe their bullshit, I will try harder and work harder; that I will don my cape and save them from the tyranny and oppression of their circumstances.

They think that I'm going to give them more of a piece of me. A piece that they really don't deserve. They say, treat me like I'm your son or a part of your family. Essentially, make my case personal to you. The irony of it all is that they never realize that I have always given too much. Every time that someone who sat next to me goes to prison, a little piece of me goes with them. It doesn't matter to me what they've been convicted of. I'm a part of that second lost life that is housed in a warehouse where prisons are placed.

How sick must I be to protect those that prey on children, the least of us? I protect those that have been predators most of their life. For them, it's always been the predator or the prey, the victim or victimizer, the rich or the poor. As ambiguous as it may seem, justice has a way of treating them all accordingly. She treats the poor as routinely as pouring herself a glass of water. However, she treats the rich like they're rich.

I never really knew that I had a calling to stand up for justice or to protect the poor and disenfranchised. It was something that was always there. When I was 16, the Mayor of Indianapolis invited my basketball team to City Hall. We were the city basketball champions. As a joke, I refused to shake the Mayor's hand. I told him that I was a Democrat. At 18, in Houston, Texas, I marched to make Martin Luther King Day a local and federal holiday. At 19, as a college athlete, I refused to eat at a Sambo's Restaurant in South Carolina because the NAACP said the name was offensive to black folks. It seemed I hadn't eaten in over 10 hours. I noticed how our coach instructed the bus driver to pass by several restaurants only to stop at Sambo's. My protest was to sit on the bus and not eat.

After nearly an hour, the black assistant coach was sent to fetch me. He told me I had made my point and that I needed to eat. I needed my strength to play in the game that night. I looked at him as if he were an Uncle Tom. How could he suggest that I eat at such a place? When I entered the restaurant, no one would look me in the eye. I believe that for most of my teammates, that was the first time they had witnessed a protest. Little did I know, my assistant coach was the first black basketball player to integrate the University of Alabama. My team never stopped at another Sambo's and Martin Luther King Day is now a part of American life.

However, today, the way that I carry myself would show you otherwise. The way I dress, walk and talk, and the car I drive is all marketing to justify why I charge so much. I must admit that I do what I do not just for the sake of justice, but also for the money. This profession allows me to live the life that I have imagined for myself. Yeah, I recognize my own hypocrisy as much as I recognize that some good people get caught up in bad situations. I accept as fact, that everyone deserves a fair trial no matter how guilty they are, which makes me different from most. The perception is that I care and I do more than most.

My one-man-upmanship attitude was fostered somewhere on my journey of life. I don't rightly know where I picked up this habit or need of wanting to win at all costs. I guess, however, that winning at all costs is ingrained in most of us who seek success on some level. Some say, it's the American way. Somehow, it all seems very trite and shallow to me, much like the gambler that loses everything only to live to play just one more time.

I am trapped in a profession that gives me license to play with people's lives. To play with life, for the sake of allowing a sick fuck to go recommit the same crime all over again and get paid for it. However, I tell myself, if he does recommit, that's between him and God. Yeah, I rationalized my fear away. I'm trapped because I don't know what else to do with my life. However, don't feel sorry for me. I'm trapped much like a henpecked man. Like him, I want to be there and it 'ain't hurting me bad enough to leave.

I play for the sake of getting over against the odds that were set in motion by a sick fuck. Sadly, I am defined on how passionately I carry out this dusty, fungus-ridden, two-faced craft called the law.

I am respected by many for the stories that I've imagined and articulated as facts. Where did I pick this thing up? For those who patiently taught me, did they know where I would take this thing? Did they see in me a moral bankruptcy that equipped me for the job? Do they really trust me or do they trust me because of what I've already shown them and that is the sheer number of murderers and rapists I've already walked.

Here we go again, another murderer and rapist sitting to my right. I first met Riddle in the Fulton County Jail. He stood during our initial visit and interview. I knew to sit and to give Riddle the perception of authority over me. I was confident enough in what I knew of his rapist's profile that I would eventually get his attention. I was trained by some of the best prosecutors in the country when

I lived and worked in Chicago. Therefore, I knew that after I used a combination of macho phrases and curse words in a sentence with legal stuff, he would soon follow my lead.

Riddle was a classic rapist in that he needed to be in control at all times. Riddle believed that all women came on to him, that he was the prize sought and not she. Riddle told me that he never came on to a woman because he didn't have to.

Riddle had been to prison for raping and butt fucking two other homeless prostitutes before I began to represent him. Seemingly, something would happen between Riddle and the women that would justify or oblige him to rape them. This whole 'she-brought-it-on-herself' thing was either she smoked up my crack and didn't want to put out, or she failed to repay money he had loaned to her on time, so Riddle had to rape her. It was always something that obliged him to fuck someone, to rape.

Riddle was about 42 years old. He had a round face with an unkempt mustache. At one time, you could tell that he was an athlete and had a muscular build. He got upset when a detective during the trial referred to him as pudgy. Riddle stood about 5'10" with his shoulders held back. This made him taller than what he actually was. His eyes were close to his nose, which made him appear to be psychotic and violent. It was just like when you see those same eyes in a movie, you know that's the crazy one.

With his booming chest thrusted forward and his direct but broken English, Riddle wanted everyone to know that he was a man. His loud raspy voice made it impossible for him to whisper. Riddle knew how to use his voice like a weapon. His breath smelled of stale baloney and morning breath. Dried mustard usually stayed in the creases of his mouth. Riddle had no concept of personal space. As I counseled with him before, during and after trial, you could smell his breath through his skin.

Riddle was a prideful homeless man that thought women were only here to create havoc in the lives of men and to be fucked. I guess he felt that we bonded because at times, he could tell I felt the same way — my divorce.

The difference, however, is that civilized men rationalize their thoughts before they act. Men are supposed to have some self-discipline or control. To the contrary, animals act in the Id, the moment. I'm hungry therefore I scavenge or kill for food. I'm horny therefore I take sex by any means necessary. In my work, sometimes it's hard to tell the difference between some people and animals.

Riddle stalked, cornered, and raped three women that I knew about. During this period of time, over 20 women had been raped and murdered in the same areas that Riddle would frequent. There was no confusion about who Riddle was or was not; he was a predator. He was possibly my second or third serial killer.

As with all things, when people get tired of losing, they figure out a way to win, even if it means cheating. In Riddle's case, he'd figured to just stop leaving witnesses. Before the days of DNA, one could rape and potentially get away with it. Then, it was all about whether or not the victim could identify the person who raped her. Sadly, there were a number of people wrongfully convicted.

In Georgia, one could be put to death for rape. This law was to put all black men on notice that if you messed with a white woman, you could be put to death. This law is still on the books but not applied without an appending murder. Don't be foolish to believe that Emmett Till was the only one.

Today, DNA will get your ass one way or the other. It's no longer necessary if a rapist can or cannot be identified by a victim. Certainly it helps, but if she said she was raped and your sperm was found inside of her vagina, your only defense was that she consented to the sex. Thus, it helps if you knew the victim's name.

For Riddle, in the mid- to late 1980's DNA evidence was new and still developing. However, over the next 10 years, DNA science would take the guesswork out of identifying who raped whom. Today, it's just a matter of whether the sex was consensual or not. If your stuff was found inside a victim, the predator now has to explain the circumstances of how it got there. The flying sperm defense has not been tried yet. My educated guess is, even if it were tried, it wouldn't work. Thus, the predator finds himself usually conceding to the science; the "she gave me the pussy" defense.

Before Riddle was released from prison on the two prior rapes, a sample of bodily fluids was taken from him for testing. Periodically, Georgia will take DNA samples from unsolved murders and run them through the DNA data bank of convicted felons. If a match is found, then all the samples are retested to confirm the initial results or findings. It took over 12 years for the District Attorney of Atlanta to find additional funding to have old DNA samples tested and matched with the prison data bank. But it happened.

In 1995, a homeless prostitute was found underneath the crawl space of an abandoned burned-out home. The crawl space is the area that separates the house from the foundation. The crawl space was about three feet high from the ground. Her body was found in an area that was shit-infested and muddy, with used condoms and crack sacks littered and strewn about. She was just in her twenties with so much life left to live.

She had been battered about the head, face, and body. Her black eyes were unmistakable. You could almost tell from just looking at the injuries that she had been struck by a man. She had blond hair and she only weighed 112 pounds. Her body had been dragged, indicated by the skin burns that were left on each hipbone. Tattered with dirt and loose bags of used crack cocaine sacks, she was dead. The peace sign on the front of the pelvis was of no avail. And yes, she had been raped.

She was found in an area of the city that was all black and crack-infested. Her blond hair made her an easy target for the homeless crackhead predators looking for an easy win. She was like a fly in a glass of milk, a mouse in a glue trap. The only thing that made her different from the scared mouse was that she was fearless. She was too trusting in that she would venture out alone in the wee hours of the morning. She hung out near or around four rooming houses where homeless crackheads, recovering addicts, and convicts lived.

When her body was found, it was amazing how all of these crackheads knew nothing about her death. Typically, crackheads know everything about everything. They are the Huggie Bears of the world, willing and ready to provide information to the police for a few dollars. However, they were all rather silent regarding the girl's death. All anyone knew was that the white girl was from Florida and that she liked to get high. The crackheads told police that the white girl would do anything for two dollars worth of stuff.

The night before her death, some saw the girl with "Lady Dee," a dike who thought she was a pimp. Lady Dee denied trying to pimp the white girl. However, it was more than a coincidence to me that Lady Dee and "Shorty the Hustler" found the white girl's body.

When I saw the victim's senior picture, commonly referred to in the business as her "in life photo," I saw this little girl, a daddy's girl, with innocence and promise in her smile. In the end, her father refused the free airline ticket and hotel room to attend the trial of the person who killed his daughter. I wondered what she did to make him abandon her even in death. Did it just hurt him so badly that she had become a crackhead prostitute or was it his guilt? Was it the guilt of another impotent man not being able to save his own daughter? Or was he part of her problem and that's why she started using drugs in the first place?

Detective Rodriguez was the new lead detective. He was articulate and detailed. Rodriguez was also a professional hostage negotiator. His Hollywood looks made it difficult to pick a jury with females. He stood about 6'2," slender but muscular, like a runner. His hair was coifed to the back with a slight fade on the sides. He hailed from Puerto Rico or South America somewhere, but he did not have a Spanish accent.

He could live the life of a Latin lover, if he wanted. In fact, I think one of the jurors tried to fuck him. He was so smooth that he could charm the panties off a polar bear. However, this was not the first time I had to dance with Rodriguez. I knew I had to be on top of my game with him. Both of us like the sport of law. It keeps it interesting for us. Plus, as compared to me, he's so fucking likable.

Rodriguez knew from his investigation that Riddle slept on an abandoned sofa behind a liquor store on Peachtree Street and worked as a picketer for a local union a few blocks from where he slept. Riddle and the other homeless people would receive free meals at a local church downtown at 7 a.m., 1 p.m., and 6 p.m. daily. When he first went to find Riddle, Rodriguez was unable to find him, but left word for him to contact police; and Riddle did.

Rodriguez advised Riddle of his rights and Riddle stated that he understood his rights. Riddle wanted to know why he was being questioned and commenced to cussing everyone out. Rodriguez began to ask Riddle about the white girl. Riddle denied knowing her at least 30 times over three interviews that lasted several hours. However, Riddle did admit that he was familiar with the location of where her body was found.

As a lawyer, I'd wish that people under suspicion for a crime would just shut the fuck up. Your silence may cause you a few days in jail, but for my clients, that's compared to life in prison without parole.

Rodriguez went on to ask Riddle that if he didn't know the white girl, why was his semen found in her butt? All of a sudden, Riddle's amnesia faded away. He recalled fucking the white girl in exchange for crack. The sex was consensual. Riddle also admitted that he'd fuck the girl in the area where her body was found, but not underneath the house, where her body was recovered.

Riddle told Rodriguez "I didn't kill nobody," that he didn't remember the white girl because he had fucked maybe a thousand white women and there was nothing special about the white girl that was found dead.

At trial, Detective Cousin, who investigated the case as the lead detective 12 years ago, described the crawl space. He remembered a number of facts over the past 12 years because on the day he arrived at the crime scene, he was wearing a new suit. He said the last thing he wanted to do was to crawl around in that feces and mud in his new suit.

After the white girl was found dead, word on the street was that Shorty was the last person seen with the white girl at about 3 a.m. Shorty was a self -proclaimed hustler from South Georgia. Shorty had already killed a man in North Carolina. However, police found that killing was in self-defense. I say after your first killing, the other ones become easier. Also, Shorty was homeless along with Lady Dee, the pimp from Arkansas, and both had been seen with the white girl within hours of her death.

Shorty admitted that he had fucked the white girl for a hit of crack, but he fucked her at least two days before she was found dead. Like Riddle, he admitted that he had fucked her in the same area where her body was found but in the neighboring abandon house. He couldn't recall if he had used a condom or not.

For some reason, Shorty the Hustler said he left the clothes he was wearing when he was with the white girl at another abandoned house. When he returned for his clothes, they had been stolen. I said that homeless people don't just leave their clothes lying around for someone to take them. I said that they would wear all of their shit first before they'd leave 'em.

I knew that Shorty had gotten rid of the clothes and shoes he was wearing when he was with the white girl. I knew that Shorty up and buried that shit somewhere in the neighborhood. Unfortunately for Riddle, the witness that last saw Shorty with the white girl had died of Aids years before the case was brought to trial, and the DNA found underneath the white girl's fingernails was not enough to identify her killer or exclude Riddle.

The trial lasted maybe two weeks. The jury failed to convict Riddle after three days of deliberation. I was able to convince at least one person that Lady Dee and Shorty could have killed the white girl.

The fact that the first jury failed to convict Riddle gave his ass a false since of security. A month or so passed before we began the second trial. Jurors from the first trial showed up in support of the state, including the juror I believe was or trying to fuck Rodriguez. You should have seen them acting like they were afraid to even speak to me. I spoke anyway.

Again, we tried the case for two weeks. Prior to trial, I told Riddle that if the state asked him to demonstrate how he had choked the other two rape victims, he's to refuse. At the first trial, Riddle told the state that he would be glad to demonstrate how he had choked his victims. Riddle commenced to choking this life size dummy with much zeal and glee. One could think that this demonstration provided Riddle with sexual pleasure. Of course, this time I wanted to avoid such a demonstration at all costs.

Nonetheless, Riddle was convicted. The first jury began to applaud the second jury for doing what they were unable to do. In both the first and second trial, we had to concede to the science of DNA. Riddle told the jury that after he had fucked the white girl, they got up and walked back in the direction of one of the many labor pools in the area.

If this were so, the anus being just like any other muscle, expands and contracts itself with certain activities. Thus, if you were to insert a penis inside the anus, it would indeed expand itself to accommodate the penis. On the other hand, once the penis is removed, the anus naturally contracts itself to its natural state.

Accepting this as a scientific and natural fact, if Riddle and the white girl were walking around after he penetrated her anus, her anus would have contracted itself upon her walking around. However, Riddle's sperm was found pooled in the white girl's ass. It's not like the sperm had seeped down her leg as gravity would have it or dried itself on her inner thighs.

At the autopsy, her anus was still dilated and the sperm was found in a nice little pool. This means she died during the sex or shortly thereafter. The medical examiner couldn't really tell us if she was already dead when he fucked her. He could only say that it was close in time. Gotcha! Whenever I drive by the Georgia Aquarium, I think of the white girl. Her body was found where the

Aquarium now stands. What a tombstone.

Riddle wrote me a letter from prison in which he refers to me as "Pimping." All of these years of educating and grooming myself to look and act the part of lawyer man, this ignorant, homeless motherfucker can still see through me.

Riddle told me that the two female prosecutors wanted to fuck him. In fact, the black prosecutor showed him her pussy during the trial. Riddle said that the white prosecutor wants to be black so badly that she's forgotten how to be herself. Riddle even told me that the judge wanted to fuck him. He told me that he could have all three of them bitches if he was on the street.

Sadly, Riddle truly believes that these successful, educated women would just love to fuck his homeless ass. Riddle, the lover that sleeps on the sofa behind the liquor store on Peachtree Street. Riddle me that.

Sentence: Life in prison without the possibility of parole.

Chapter 5

Jealousy

A SONG FOR TRE

He was only three years old when he arrived from the Virgin Islands. His mother, Shawanda, left him with his father before he was even a year old. Shawanda had moved to Atlanta. Tre was beautiful. He was small for his age but he was beautiful. Tre had this caramel complexion, curly hair, and a winning smile. As Tre got older, he was destined for special treatment in life. People love to be around beautiful people. Tre was going to be a part of the Beautiful People Fraternity.

Tre had only been in Atlanta for three months. In those three months, he was rushed to the emergency room three times. The last time he was rushed to the hospital, he died. In three months, Tre had suffered a fractured arm and bruised hip that caused him to walk with a limp. Finally, someone had punched or kicked Tre in the stomach so hard that it caused his stomach to press against his spine.

The medical examiner found 17 identifiable injuries on Tre's body. His internal injuries included a contusion to the right side of his head in the temple area, where blood was found just underneath the skin. Tre had another internal contusion to his stomach that matched the area where he had been kicked or punched. This injury had crushed his spleen and lacerated his bowels. I can't imagine how painful the bowel slippage was. All of this happened in just three months.

Shawanda had finally sent for Tre when she thought she was ready to be a mother. Up until this time, his father and his girlfriend of the month were rearing Tre. Seemingly, Tre's dad would always find a woman that already had kids. For most of his three years of life, Tre was treated like an unwanted orphan. His needs would come second after everyone else. My father would tell me the same thing after his mother died when he was only six years old. His father remarried a woman with children. My father felt helpless when his stepbrother would fuck his sister. He never accepted the fact that he was too young to help. He never considered the possibility that his sister just wanted to be fucked.

Shawanda was short and fat. She had become ghettoized since she'd been here. Ghettoized in a way where she had abandoned the customs and ways of her native Caribbean roots. Much like black women who've abandoned any semblance of African culture for that of white women, Shawanda sported a geometric hairstyle with the long fingernails. Her nails were so long that she had limited use of her hands because her nails were curled underneath her hand. With those fingernails, I'm sure Shawanda had trouble wiping her own ass. I have often wondered where ghetto girls get their fashion sense. Who convinces them that blue or orange hair is attractive? Why do they desecrate their bodies with tattoos of tigers, panthers, and Asian symbols they don't really understand? It was clear to me that Shawanda had assimilated beyond the mainstream American idiom. She jumped right into American ghetto culture. Sadly, Shawanda thought this was cute.

Shawanda was very proud of her relationship with David. On the other hand, she was very insecure about their relationship. It was quite obvious that he was using her. Also, it was quite obvious that

David was a kept man. David had not worked in over a year. He, Shawanda, and Tre all shared an apartment with David's brother, James. James had worked 10 years at a national airline carrier as a baggage handler. James and Shawanda shared the rent and utilities. She would buy food for David and Tre. James would buy his own food. Shawanda also gave David an allowance whenever she'd get paid from Kroger, the grocery store where she worked as a cashier.

Both David and Shawanda had cars. However, the car seat was kept in Shawanda's car. David would drive her car for family concerns, like going to the grocery store, taking Shawanda to work, and things like that. David would only drive his car when he wanted to cruise and hang out with his boys.

David was a catch for Shawanda. He was about 6'1" tall and weighed 190 pounds. He worked as a professional trainer for a while and you could tell he kept himself up. With broad shoulders, flat abs, and a lean physique, David was a looker. He sported a short fade hairstyle and kept a trimmed mustache. This all contrasted nicely with his brown complexion and his long eyelashes. When he spoke of happier times back home, his baritone Caribbean accent could cause you to daydream. He too was from the U.S. Virgin Islands.

I met David through his cousin, who was a lady friend of Caribbean descent. David's cousin worked in the Courthouse system. I am always humbled when such people contact me to represent a friend or relative. It is validation. See, courthouse personnel, judges, bailiffs, and court reporters all know which lawyers are competent and which ones are not. They see lawyers every day, year-in and year-out. However, if you are not on top of your game, they label you as an idiot. Sadly, you may stay an idiot your entire career in their eyes.

I never liked trying certain cases, especially those involving child molesters and rapists. I especially don't like representing people who are accused of killing babies. But, on any given day, I will sign up a client accused of such acts depending on how broke

I am. However, if I'm holding some cheese, my fee goes up. If the client wanted to hire me anyway at the higher fee, so be it. If he finds someone cheaper, that's fine too. When David's case came through the door, I was broke.

It's hard for people not to prejudge someone that's accused of killing a baby. I'm no different. I know from experience that baby killers usually involve a jealous boyfriend or a step dad. Child molesters are also included in this class. I know that some parents do kill their own, much like some animals eat their young, but that doesn't happen as often.

David cried when we first met. At this point in my life, I still can't separate tears of sorrow from those of guilt. I try very hard not to become too cynical, but I'm tired of being played by my clients. This shit is emotional enough without allowing another motherfucker on my roller coaster. Anyway, David was a boyfriend and I couldn't sit my suspicions of him down.

Early on in my investigation of the case, I knew that I was dealing with an incompetent police investigation. Moreover, the more I learned about Shawanda, the clearer it was that her temper was a lot meaner than David's.

David told me that he was not allowed to discipline Tre. The one time he did at the grocery store, Shawanda cursed him out and called him all kinds of motherfuckers and shit. Embarrassed, David left the store with his tail between his legs. It didn't matter to Shawanda that other customers were around and that they were in public.

Even still, Shawanda knew that David fucked around on her. She would even catch him cheating on her from time to time, but it didn't stop shit. She'd still pay half the bills to James and she still would give David an allowance. When Shawanda would catch David cheating, she'd just act out. One time she threw a lamp at his head. The lamp left a hole in the wall after it broke into two pieces. On another occasion, when David was dressing to go out, Shawanda smashed the front windshield of David's car with her fist.

She cracked his front windshield with her bare hands. I didn't think this was even possible for a man to do, let alone a woman. Of course when Shawanda would get upset, she'd take it out on Tre.

I was able to get David out of jail on bond. A friend of a friend was the sitting judge. David just had to surrender his passport. As soon as David was released from jail, he brought me the pictures of the broken lamp, the hole in the wall, and a picture of the shattered windshield. He told me that he received a call from Shawanda.

Obviously, I told him to stay away from her, that his bond could be revoked and his ass could end up back in jail. He said that he would. But I knew he had already fucked her. He denied it. I told him, I know you fucked her and don't do it again. Again, he denied fucking her. David had been in jail six months. He gets out and this trick, whose baby he's accused of killing, is calling him.

Conversely, she may not have had any dick in six months. I doubt it, but it's possible. David gets out of jail and she fucks him just like that. She's fucked and Tre is merely an afterthought. At first, the pussy started out awkward, but it came around to itself for a moment. Just like when you fuck an ex-wife or girlfriend after a few years of divorce or separation. Seemingly, in that moment, it was awkward again. If not for you, it certainly was for her.

As we wrapped up our conversation and David was about to leave, I told him not to fuck her again. David smiled like a mischievous child and told me that he wouldn't. David tried to lie to me about some pussy. I was a recovering whore well before I met him. You know we all know who we are. An addict can spot another addict from across a crowded room in the dark. I wondered what else David had lied to me about.

At trial, it was brought up that David told police that the only thing unusual about the day's events was that Tre had a fall in the tub. The police turned that statement around into an accusation that Tre died because he had fallen in the tub. Obviously, the medical examiner refuted that story. The medical examiner made it clear that such a fatal injury could not have occurred from a fall in the tub.

Tre's spleen had turned into soup. The medical examiner concluded that Tre had either been punched or kicked in the stomach. The contusion on his stomach was the size of a fist. Tre died of blunt force trauma to the stomach.

Shawanda had no explanation for any of Tre's injuries; the fractured arm, bruised hip, and the fatal blow to the stomach — no explanation. She told the jury that the scratches that littered Tre's body from head to toe were self-inflicted. She told the jury that David kept Tre during the day while she worked all the time. She didn't know anything because she was at work all the time. Shawanda did admit that she did not allow David to discipline Tre. She also stated that Tre would have told on David if he had spanked him.

Shawanda confirmed the grocery store incident when she did curse David out in public for the one time he disciplined Tre. She also admitted to smashing David's windshield with her fist. As Shawanda testified, no tears fell from her eyes. I asked her, of all of these injuries to Tre, you don't have an answer for any of them? Again, she told me no. I asked her, "What about when you would bathe Tre, you didn't see the scratches all over his body?" Again, she replied, no. David would bathe Tre most of the time. However, when she did bathe him, she didn't see any marks or scratches on his body.

When Shawanda's mother, Betty, got on the witness stand, you could see where Shawanda got her name. Her mother was just as ghetto-fabulous as she. Betty confirmed for the jury what I already knew. In the three months that Tre was here, she didn't spend much time with him. Betty had four additional kids besides Shawanda and she had a new boyfriend. Thus, she wasn't trying to be a grandmother.

Betty was only in her forties and the new boyfriend she met at the club was more important to her than celebrating a grandbaby. Shit, she got kids at home. Betty also sported a long ponytail weave and fake nails. She had referred to the new boyfriend as her fiancé even though they had only met a few months ago. I mean it can happen, but to me the boyfriend was just another nigga she met at the club.

Betty blamed everything on David. She claimed that Tre was with David when Tre got ill. David was the caretaker while Shawanda was at work. Tre was with David when his hip was injured and when he fractured his arm. David, David, David. I reminded her that Tre's arm was injured while at her house with his badass uncles.

I wanted to know, where were you, Ms. Betty, when Tre needed his grandmother? Besides, the medical examiner told the jury that Tre would not have lasted for long with the type of injuries he suffered to his stomach. Again, the fall in the tub occurred that morning, or at most, early afternoon. Something happened in that car.

The police, however, failed to scoop up Tre's vomit from the car or parking lot of the apartment complex to have it tested. This evidence could have given clues of what was expelled from Tre within hours of his death. The receipt from the grocery store could have shed light on why Shawanda and David sought to purchase the medicine for Tre and compared that with the time they entered the hospital. Tre's underwear wasn't recovered as evidence. In all, we had no crime scene in Tre's case because the police failed to identify one. Like me, they wanted to conclude that it's always the boyfriend or step dad who commits the crime. Consequently, they did nothing.

When David testified, he explained to the jury the pictures of violence caused by Shawanda that he had given to me. David told the jury how he and Tre would dress alike. How he'd buy matching outfits for the both of them with the money Shawanda would give him. You could tell that David liked it when people would ask him if Tre was his son.

David described to the jury how Tre cried because he was tired and hungry on the drive home from Shawanda's job. They lived

30 miles south of Buckhead, where Shawanda worked. In traffic, it could take over an hour to get home. It was a Friday, and David told Shawanda that he was going to hang out with his boys and that he needed his allowance. Shawanda became upset with him because he was late picking her up from work and now he wants money to go out. They argued back and forth as Tre became more irritable.

As David drove into their apartment complex, he stopped at the mailbox to check the mail. The mailbox was out of view from the car. When he returned to the car, Tre had vomited in the car and soiled himself. David explained how he took Tre from Shawanda and walked to the apartment. There, he cleaned Tre up and soaked his soiled underwear in the sink. Tre layed down for a minute and they tried to give him some juice, which he threw up.

They decided to get some medicine at the grocery store. The store was less than a mile away from the apartment. David made the purchase while Shawanda stayed in the car with Tre. When David returned with the medicine, Tre threw up the medicine as well. David left the store and then drove to the hospital. Less than an hour later, Tre was dead.

David cried as he explained that he believed that Shawanda punched Tre while he went to the mailbox. This was interesting to me because Shawanda never accused David of injuring Tre. She simply went along with how everything looked. I now feel that she fucked David when he got out of jail, just to keep him quiet. You know, some hush pussy. I didn't confront her with fucking David while he was out on bond because I think Shawanda's fate was already sealed with the jury even though she was not the one on trial.

We need to know that our children are safe; that parents will protect their own children and we, as a society, will do our best to help or have their backs in every way. This is so whether it is in crime prevention and prosecution or healthcare. Shawanda had failed Tre and the jury was angry with her.

David had several childhood friends that flew in from the Virgin

Islands, New York, and here in Atlanta. They all vouched for David as a true Caribbean man. Seemingly, nothing bothered David, as he was so laid back and nonchalant — but not in a pretentious way. David was just cool. He just had a certain peace about him. In everything with David, his response was the same – "no problem man."

The jury chose to believe David's friends. Shawanda had already admitted to them how violent she could be. David was found not guilty of Tre's murder and not guilty on all counts. To date, no one has been charged with Tre's murder.

As I left the courthouse, Shawanda was sitting on a bench outside of the courtroom. As I walked by her, she lunged at me calling me all kinds of black motherfuckers. I guess I deserved it; I did accuse her of killing her baby. Her 19-year-old brother was waiting for me outside the courthouse. I guess once he saw me up close, standing 6'3" and weighing 270 pounds, he figured that I was not an easy win by himself. He, too, called me a motherfucker and bloodclot bumblebee. I didn't know what the fuck he was talking about. I just kept walking. Ironically, none of Shawanda's people said anything to David, the man accused and acquitted of killing their loved one.

Two years later, David brought his 6-month old son by his new woman to my office. We laughed, talked, and basically caught up with each other. The baby was beautiful; he looked so much like Tre to me.

SALT

"Jealousy in relationships is like salt is to food...a little salt enhances the taste...too much salt drowns the flavor and sometimes kills you."

— Dr. Maya Angelo

Blue had moved to Atlanta with dreams of getting his rap career off the ground. After a year of suffering in the Broadway of the south, Blue found himself homeless and nearly broke. Then he met Ray Davis. Ray was a leasing agent at a local apartment complex. Even though Ray told Blue he failed to qualify for an apartment, he would rent Blue a room at his house. Blue told me he prayed the Lord would guide and instruct him. He prayed that the Lord would give him a place to stay and the Lord did. He led him to Ray.

Ray was married with a five-month old son. Only 26 years old and recently discharged from the military, Ray and his wife were trying to make ends meet themselves. He was from California and he had no real family here. His wife was unemployed and Ray needed Blue's rent money just as badly as Blue needed a place to live. On the surface, it seemed like a win-win situation for Ray and Blue. God does answer prayers.

Blue paid Ray $200 in advance to cover two weeks of rent before he moved a mattress and his clothes into the house. Ray laid out some house rules, which Blue agreed to, and everything appeared as if it would work out. That was before Ray killed himself.

Blue told police that after he rented the room from Ray, he would call him on his job every day. At first, Blue said the calls were no big deal, but after the second and third call on consecutive days, Blue told a co-worker. Blue began to think Ray was concerned that Blue would be home alone with his wife while he was at work or school. Ray attended a community college at night and was taking some remedial classes to prepare for a mainstream college.

On the date in question, Blue told police he had spent the night at a friend's house and left there for work. While at work, Ray called him again and asked him about his night. Blue simply told him he had spent the night with a friend, but would be home later that night. When Blue made it home, Ray was not there. Blue said he felt something was amidst, so he asked Mrs. Davis if everything was all right with him living there. Mrs. Davis said that everything was fine. Blue then asked Mrs. Davis if she wanted anything from the store, and left.

Blue stated when he returned from the store, he prepared to cut up some chicken wings with a butcher's knife from the kitchen. As he prepared to cook, Mrs. Davis told him things were not okay between her and her husband. She explained that since she was out of work, they were having financial trouble. Mrs. Davis also told Blue that Ray was a very jealous man, but had calmed down sense the birth of their son. In the past, Ray had a problem with his friends coming onto his girlfriends. As Blue told Mrs. Davis about the repeated calls to his job, Ray abruptly comes out of a bedroom and began to argue with both Blue and his wife.

Ray chastised his wife for telling Blue that he was a jealous man and argued with Blue, suggesting that if Blue had a problem with the calls, Blue should have spoken to him man to man. Blue said that it wasn't long before Ray pushed his wife and son out of the kitchen area, and was yelling in his face — nose to nose. Neither Blue nor Mrs. Davis knew that Ray was home. It appeared that Ray had snuck inside the house and didn't want to be detected. It also appeared that Ray was eavesdropping on their conversation. Blue said that Ray confronted him, while the knife was in his hands. At some point, Mrs. Davis got between the two of them and pleaded with them to calm down. Mrs. Davis said that Blue told her he wouldn't do anything to hurt her husband because of her and the baby. But he refused to set the knife down. He was afraid of what Ray might do.

After both Blue and Mrs. Davis asked him to calm down, Ray only became more irate during the course of the argument. Ray then told Blue he was jealous of him because he was younger than Blue — even though he was renting from Ray. Ray then told Blue he had to leave the house. He was being evicted. Blue told Ray that that was fine, but he wanted Ray to refund one week of the rent money because he had stayed only a week.

Ray left the kitchen and headed toward his bedroom supposedly to retrieve Blue's money. Blue positioned himself in the hallway that was between the bedroom and an exit to the house. Blue said he took the knife that he was using from the kitchen with him because Ray's behavior was so unpredictable. As Blue waited on Ray to return with his money, Blue assured Mrs. Davis that he was not going to injure Ray, he just wanted his money back and he would leave.

When Ray returned, he saw the knife was still in Blue's hand and became angry again. Ray called Blue weak, and said he didn't like Niggas from Virginia anyway. Ray approached Blue and grabbed him by his wrists, before Ray headbutted him in the mouth. The headbutt injured Blue's lip and forced Blue to bite through his tongue. A struggled ensued between the Blue and Ray, when the knife punctured Ray in the leg.

Ray soon realized he had been stabbed, and told his wife to call 911. Mrs. Davis became so hysterical that she couldn't find her cell phone. A hysterical Blue then called 911. When the operator told him, "Ma'am, ma'am, please calm down." Blue exclaimed, "I'm a man." Blue then removed Ray's shorts, wrapped a towel around Ray's wound, and applied pressure. Sadly, by the time paramedics arrived, Ray had bled to death and Blue was charged with his murder.

As Blue sat in the little interview room waiting to be questioned by police, Blue raised his hands to the ceiling and he asked God, "How do I get this off of my soul? What will happen to this little boy who will grow up without a father? Lord help me. Lord help this child." With his busted lip and Ray's blood on his shirt, pants, and shoes, Blue began to cry.

The homicide cop questioned Blue about what had occurred. Blue told him the same story Ray's wife told him. But the detective kept prefacing his questions to Blue with, "After you stabbed him." Blue asked him to stop saying it like that. Blue told police Ray was injured as they tussled and Ray headbutted him. Blue claimed he never attempted to cut or stab Ray. The medical examiner testified that Ray's injury could have occurred just like Blue said it did.

Mrs. Davis testified that Blue was in fact jealous of her husband because he was older than Ray yet needed to rent from them. As I questioned her, I just let her say whatever she wanted to say. Eventually, I asked her if she told Blue that her husband was a jealous man. She replied yes, but only in response to Blue questioning the living situation. I asked her if she did anything that was disrespectful to her husband. She told us how faithful she was and that Ray was her first everything. Lastly, I asked her if she and Blue were having an inappropriate conversation before Ray entered the room all upset. She said, "No, we weren't talking about nothing."

"So, your husband became so upset over nothing?" I asked.

She replied, "Yes, yes he did."

I told Mrs. Davis that it wasn't her fault, but she wouldn't look at me. I told her again and again before she looked at me and physically resigned from further questioning. Her body language told us that her husband at the end of the day was a man consumed by his own insecurities, his past, and too much salt.

Blue's murder charges were dismissed.

ANGEL EYES

He told her he was going to kill her when he got out of jail. This time, it appeared that she took him seriously because she went to stay with Mr. Mack. Mr. Mack was about 70 years old and bound to a wheelchair. He lived in one of those federally subsidized high-rise housing projects for the disabled. I don't know what his disability was, but I knew he liked to take a taste of brown liquor from time to time.

Mr. Mack allowed Celeste to stay with him right before Hank was released from jail. I don't know how Celeste and Mr. Mack knew each other, but it appeared that he was kind to her. I don't know if Celeste had any living parents or family support. I do know that she had three kids — either two with Hank and one with another man, or one with Hank and two with someone else. Celeste and Hank had been together close to 20 years. Hank considered Celeste to be his common law wife.

Both Hank and Celeste were crackheads. Although I know they didn't start out that way, it would be presumptuous of me to suggest they had a shot at life like everyone else. I just don't know if they did or not.

I met Celeste in a photograph. She was dead, but her eyes were still open. As I looked at Celeste's photographs, I thought her eyes separated her thoughts of pain, desperation, and death. I thought that Hank had finally done it. He had sneaked his way into Mr. Mack's apartment building where he met a surprised Celeste. She was exiting the elevator when he stabbed her the first time. Hank saw Celeste before she saw him. There was no place for her to run. Hank stabbed Celeste 30 times. He stabbed her all over her body until the knife broke. Hank stabbed her in front of a nine-year-old girl and the girl's father. Yes, right there in the lobby of Mr. Mack's apartment building. Hank continued to stab and jab Celeste with that butcher knife. He stabbed her as she screamed and fell to the floor. The nigga even stabbed her behind her knees so she couldn't run.

As I looked at the crime scene photos of Celeste, I could see her smooth brown skin. She wasn't as dark as me. Her hair appeared to be slicked back with Vaseline. Her eyes were round, but not almond-shaped. They appeared to be bulging from her eye sockets. I don't know if her eyes were like that when she was alive. One goes through a lot of changes when they face death. See, for each of us, death has its own face.

Sometimes, to look at the photos of the deceased before the makeup is on or the hair is groomed is one thing. But to see death in its natural state may tell us a story of how they lived. However, some say how you die has nothing to do with how you lived. They use the crucifixion of Jesus as an example. I say that skinny people have heart attacks too.

However, looking through that window of mortality, one finds oneself trying to discern answers to one's own life. What would your last thoughts be after you realize that death is here? Do you wonder if you are worthy of going to a better place or if you will find peace as we understand it to be or should you be afraid? Are you or is anyone ever ready for death? Did you do enough on earth to show yourself approved to God or were you merely a Sunday Worshiper? Were you a convenient Christian because you were too afraid to be anything else?

I wondered if Celeste was tired of living in fear of Hank or in fear of her addiction. In these photos, I looked at her as closely as I could to see if she could tell me her story through her expression of death. I studied Celeste's photos looking for understanding, but I didn't find it. I know some of us seek resolution in death because it's too hard to live our own life. Hank either decided or convinced himself that Celeste could not live without him being in her life. So, he killed her. I guess being the cheap nigga that he was, he was too stingy to just kill himself and leave her alone.

The photo marked state's exhibit 1 was a picture of Celeste lying in the floor with her dress above her waist and her panties showing. The photo marked state's exhibit 2 was the broken knife used to kill Celeste by her side. The knife handle had been broken off in the attack. My mother would tell my father that she would stab his no good ass, twist the blade, and break off the handle. She would say this after she'd catch him cheating on her. Regretfully, she never did. However, I guess my life is better knowing my mother didn't kill my father, even if he did deserve it.

I first met Hank in the holding cell outside of the courtroom. Hank was a slim man in his forties that looked homeless. Hank sported a shaved head and he was my complexion, a shade above midnight. Hank even sounded like a crackhead. When he spoke, his words all ran together. He told me that he didn't know anything about Celeste's murder. Hank told me he was innocent. Naturally, I agreed with him. I told him that all of my clients start out that way. Hank didn't find my sense of humor funny.

I told Hank that his case had been continued. Hank then asked me, "Whenwegocourtgin?" I guess the look on my face said it all when Hank cleared his throat and asked, "When do we go to court again?" I told him I didn't know. Hank wanted me to bring his discovery when I came to visit him in jail. Hank specifically requested that I bring the photos of Celeste at the crime scene.

The discovery is a package of materials that included police reports and summaries of the various police officers' investigation. Included in the discovery would be lab tests that were done for drug use detection, crime scene photos, and the autopsy report.

At that moment, I asked Hank why he wanted Celeste's photos in death. He told me that they were his. Plus, he wanted to assist me in his defense. I told Hank since he wasn't there at the time Celeste was murdered that he didn't need the photos of her in death. At this point, I realized that it was I who wanted to protect Celeste's privacy over the warped interest of Hank. To me, Hank didn't deserve to see Celeste in death. I rationalized that I don't like looking at these photos myself, so why would he want to see them? I asked Hank, "Where were you when Celeste was murdered?" Hank claimed he didn't know or he just wouldn't tell me.

Weeks went by, but I eventually gave Hank his discovery packet. I intentionally left the photos of Celeste out. Hank was angry with me. I asked Hank how would we explain to the jury what he did the night before the murder. How he was able to slip through the security door and make his way up to Mr. Mack's apartment. Mr. Mack told me Hank banged on his door like the police. He and Celeste knew it was Hank even though he wouldn't say anything. Mr. Mack said he and Celeste pretended not to be home.

Hank never announced himself. He just repeatedly banged on the door until another tenant threatened to call police. Hank left before police arrived. When police did arrive, Celeste told police about other officers she had talked to about Hank.

A determined Hank returned that same evening and banged on the door. This time, Mr. Mack let him in. Hank searched the house like a mad man, looking for Celeste. He looked in the shower, underneath beds, closets, and everywhere else. No Celeste. Mr. Mack told Hank she wasn't there, but Hank didn't believe him. I asked Hank about the note he left with Mr. Mack telling Celeste she had 24 hours to call him. Hank wouldn't talk about the case nor would he look me in the eyes. Hank told me he needed those goddamn pictures. Before I could ask him why, Hank got up and left the visit. He was shitty with me.

Weeks later, I eventually brought Celeste's crime scene photos to Hank. He refused to pull them out and discuss anything about the case with me. I asked Hank if it mattered to him that a nine-year-old girl was set to testify against him. Hank replied, "What little girl?" I told him the little girl that was with her father — the people he was able to slip into the building with.

I think Hank was so fixated on killing Celeste that he didn't even see the little girl standing near the elevator with her dad. I can't say that it would have even mattered if Hank did see the girl. Hank was there to kill Celeste, not to be polite. Again, Hank left the interview. Seemingly, I had reminded Hank of a witness he had forgotten about.

You have to wonder, just how fucked up this nine-year-old will become? Will she ever live to outrun what she saw? Does she dream about it? How did her father explain this to his little girl? Was it one of those things beyond explanation? Why would a nigga stab his wife 30 times in front of a nine-year-old or anyone for that matter? I know an explanation must be out there, however lost in the abyss of bullshit it may be.

I still think about this nine-year-old enjoying her day with her dad. They entered the building to visit a sick relative, much like Mr. Mack. She's happy because she doesn't get to see her dad a lot. He lives in Alabama. They are laughing about nothing as they entered the building, and Hank slipped into the building behind them. They don't really see anyone but each other as they waited on the elevator. They especially didn't see Hank, the homeless looking man we are taught as a society to ignore. Conversely, as a homeless man, Hank was experienced in making himself invisible.

They know Hank is there, but they don't really see him until the elevator door opens. They wait for Celeste to exit the elevator when Hank stabbed her the first time. I can see how she grabbed her father's arm and he grabbed her, pulling her toward him and out of harm's way. I can see how he held her face into his stomach, attempting to shield her eyes from the 29 additional stab wounds Hank would inflict on Celeste.

I can see her little face of curiosity stealing glances of Celeste's life and death. I imagined the little girl's eyes making contact with Celeste's eyes. Celeste may have even spoken to her with her eyes as she lay there dying. What did she tell the little girl? Did Celeste ask for prayer? Did she think the little girl was an angel?

I guess the only explanation you can give your child is that you don't want anyone who has to hit on you or you on them. See, it's never the only time. My father told my brother this when he battered his girlfriend.

Ironically, my father gave me this same advice when I was a kid. Lavern wanted to be my girlfriend. Lavern was a tomboy. She was just as tall as me, more athletic, and smarter. I told her that if she'd comb her hair, she could be my girlfriend. She chased me home when I didn't keep my word. Daddy was so upset I was running from a girl. But after I told him why, through his laughter, he gave me the aforementioned advice.

I told momma the story and at the same time, I told her that I might as well let the precocious Lavern be my girlfriend because her family was friends with our family. Momma told me that I was to never date anyone out of sympathy. If I liked them, then that was fine. But she was not to meet all of my girlfriends, only the special ones. After I told Lavern what my mother had said, I took that beat down like a man. Even though my parents are long deceased, I still live by this advice. In life, that advice has certainly given me a stronger step. Today, I would be a lucky man to have a woman like Lavern. Swans do fly.

Seemingly, for my father, the subject of abuse was something that he learned himself after inflicting years of physical and emotional abuse on my mother. Like most people, she would be ashamed and embarrassed of me sharing this private matter, but it happened. However, it is my prayer that whatever message Celeste gave little "Angel Eyes," I hope she got it.

A few weeks later, I paid Hank a visit at the county jail. Hank told me he wanted to plead guilty to Celeste's murder. I guess he just needed the proof that she was really dead. As with most clients, I would at least tell them how we could beat the case. You know, exploit the weaknesses in the state's case. This time, I didn't try to talk him out of it. I wasn't about to try to cross-examine a nine-year-old with angel eyes about her observations of Celeste's murder if I didn't have to.

Sentence: Life in prison.

BIG MAN IN A SMALL GAME

Vincente was from the bush in Jamaica. She was very attractive, tall, and athletic. When she got to the states, she was extremely humble, if not timid. However, that soon changed the longer she stayed separated from her motherland, Jamaica. Everybody that comes to America soon changes, whether their Italians, Irish, Africans, or Eastern Europeans. We all want to fit in and that's not a bad thing.

The dilemma of who we were when we got here and what we've become after the stay is what sometimes gets us into trouble. America, the great melting pot, is a place that the world wants to come to because she allows one to chase their dreams and have fun trying — the land of opportunity — well, depending on this, that, and the other.

Garmel was also from Jamaica. He was a tall ex-cop, married with five kids; three with his wife and two out of wedlock. Garmel was also an athlete. He met Vincente when she first arrived at the Atlanta University campus here in Atlanta. Vincente had been given a track scholarship to run the 400 at the AU center and Garmel had secured a track scholarship at the AU center a year before.

Garmel taught Vincente about everything from feminine protection to placing her napkin on her lap when eating in public. He was to Vincente as Dr. Henry Higgins was to Eliza Doolittle in "My Fair Lady." Garmel's approach to the naive Vincente was that of a big brother, who nurtured himself into a dirty uncle, then a homeboy, before he became an obligatory lover. Vincente agreed to the sex because he had done so much for her and she honestly thought this was a way to repay him. After awhile, it was just convenient for her, since she was lonely and so far away from home.

To have the married 25-year-old Garmel as a lover was better than being alone for the barely 18-year-old Vincente. Besides, Garmel did worship her and she came to depend on him for everything, as he wanted her to. Vincente played right into his efforts because she didn't know any better. Even if Vincente wanted to meet the other guys, she couldn't because his constant attention suffocated her.

Garmel's angle into Vincente was trust, the same angle I have used in the past to build up dependency in my relationships. Trust has always been an effective tool to use in the girl game because so many people lack it but really want it — or so they think. Older women eventually come to expect men to be men so long as they bring the check home. That's all the trust they need.

For older women, it becomes a matter of a standard of life and a way of living. Older women realize at the end of the day they value being comfortable more so than washing a man's dirty drawers. The optimism of having a man not so preoccupied with pussy is replaced with their reality of his banality. They recognize that wisdom and age runs a parallel course that only intersects when one is near death. By that time, quietly, she misses him, but she is glad his ass is gone, with the proverbial, "all he put me through" repeating itself in the back of her mind.

I too have been guilty of playing a big man in a small game. I've caught a light bill or even a mortgage payment here and there. In fact, Moses and I joke about some of the sponsorships we've had in exchange for company. To fuck with me, Moses would accuse me of buying one of my friends a house. But, it's all the same — a big man in a small game, and a big fish in a small pond. In the land of the blind, the man with one eye is king. Find the opportunity and serve it. Before long, she will feel indebted to you and want to please you.

Sometimes, it's easier to pay than to have the obligation that comes along with relationships. America is based on a quid pro quo system. Charity has always been something that occurred after you've fed yourself. No one in America really expects you to sacrifice too much too often. So, I didn't fault Garmel for playing a big man, I faulted him because he didn't realize, as he should, that Vincente would one day grow up. I fault him because he didn't have to kill her.

I got a call one summer from a friend who told me that a guy out of Houston was trying to hire me for a case. As it turned out, the guy out of Houston was actually an attorney. We competed against each other when we played college basketball. He told me his cousin was in trouble and he needed me. I told him to have his cousin to come visit with me right away and he did. Fifteen minutes later, Garmel walked into my office. It's as if Garmel was on his way, as I spoke to his cousin.

Garmel began to talk to me about the situation. Of course, Garmel, being an ex-Jamaican cop, only wanted to talk to me using hypothetical situations as a preface to each question. I didn't care. This approach helps me out as well, in case there is something about the facts I don't like, I can change them. Anyway, Garmel started telling me about a girl whose body hadn't been found, but was obviously dead. He told me that he had a past relationship with the girl for over five years and she had had five abortions for him. Garmel told me at one time he loved the girl more than he loved his wife and that he would have died for her.

When I asked him how the girl died, he said that he thinks someone choked her to death. I asked him how he knew she had been choked to death. He said he had just left her apartment. I asked him if she was already dead when he got there, and he said yes. I asked him if he saw marks around her neck. He said he didn't see any. Again, I asked how he knew she had been choked to death. Garmel went silent.

Garmel told me he had gone to Vincente's apartment to check her e-mail. "But you knew she was still at work," I said. "Yes, she was supposed to be at work," Garmel said. At this point, I knew I was dealing with a stalker. I also knew that Garmel had just left the scene of the murder and came straight to me. Vincente's body hadn't been found and no one knew she was dead except Garmel, her murderer, and possibly me. I asked Garmel if he used his cell phone while he was checking Vincente's e-mail. He assured me he hadn't. I asked when was the last time he communicated with Vincente by e-mail, and if it was recently. Before he could answer, I told Garmel that police would be looking for his computer.

I asked Garmel if he and Vincente were dating at the time she was killed and he said no, Vincente was seeing an Atlanta Police Officer. Garmel told me how he confronted the Cop outside of Sylvia's restaurant, where the cop worked a second job. Garmel also told me the night before Vincente died, the cop was to bring the clothes she had left at his place when she would spend the night. I asked Garmel how he knew all of this, and Garmel just looked at me as if to say, "I know you got it by now," as if he was in fact a stalker.

I asked Garmel if he knew of anyone else who was interested in Vincente and he told me about this older guy she had begun to jog with every day after work. He was a wealthy financier and had a Buckhead condo. Garmel said his number would probably be the last number on her voicemail because I'm sure she didn't go running that night.

Garmel wasn't the first person who killed someone and ran to me. However, he was the first person to run to me when the body was still warm and wearing the same clothes he committed the act in. I wasn't afraid or alarmed sitting with a killer. When they come to me, my mind just kicks into gear to protect them. My instinct becomes, "how do I get him off?" At the end of the day, Garmel was just a jealous man who perhaps killed his young lover because he didn't want her to fly without him.

During the five years Vincente was here, she competed on her college track team. She was training to run for the Jamaican Olympic team, as was her sister. Vincente had graduated from college. Vincente paid her money to take the GMAT in the fall, as she was seeking to further her education. At the time of her death, Vincente was working for the state Juvenile Justice Project, a program that attempted to save juveniles from becoming repeat offenders. She met the Atlanta cop one summer while on the job.

Vincente was also beautiful. She wore her hair to her shoulders. She had a medium-brown complexion, long legs, and naturally squared but soft shoulders. Vincente's face was narrow, but accentuated by her high cheekbones and full lips. The fact she was tall and physically fit made her apple-bottom ass round and perfect, like a basketball. Most importantly, at the time of her death, Vincente wasn't the naive little girl from the bush in Jamaica. She at some point realized the attention she was getting from men, and she liked it.

Garmel told me that he felt Vincente had put a spell on him that made him lose his mind. I was inclined to believe him after he confessed to tasting her blood. I also had a different opinion of Vincente, because she let him. Vincente let him because at some point she knew that he would do anything for her. For Vincente to have him to retrieve her feminine protection at crowded stores wasn't enough to emasculate him. She had to go further. I wondered if Vincente was motivated by revenge because her learning curve had changed. Vincente now remembered how Garmel had taken advantage of her naivety and her young, tender pussy. Garmel told me he bought Vincente her first box of tampons. Garmel recalled how Vincente was still using them grandma pads when he met her. We laughed. Hypothetically speaking, I told Garmel he had it bad.

I put Garmel on a plane to Jamaica before Vincente's body was found, or right after that. Garmel needed to at least get his money together for what I had already done, and to say goodbye to his identical twin, his wife, and his kids. Garmel knew without me having to tell him that the next time he'd hit American soil, he was gonna' probably stay awhile.

Vincente failed to report for work for about three days before people at her job did a welfare check at her apartment. Vincente's supervisor and the apartment management where she lived found Vincente's partially naked body hanging over the bathtub.

Her panties, still affixed to her body, were pulled down, ripped, and torn to the side, exposing her private parts, with shit between her ass. Her beautiful skin had turned black and was slipping off of her body into the tub. Someone had taken the time to close the shower curtain, but left her on her knees bending forward in to the tub and her butt in the air.

Immediately, the police secured her cell phone records and her computer. Police had the medical examiner to preserve all of her bodily fluids and waste to check for DNA. It wasn't long before police learned of Garmel.

Vincente's supervisor told police about the guy they had fired because of his constant harassment of Vincente. Vincente complained that her co-worker would break into her e-mail, check her voicemail messages without permission, and follow her around downtown during her lunch hour. They attempted to re-assign the guy, but the harassment continued, so they fired him. His name was Garmel.

When the story of Vincente's death hit the news, police had placed a "bolo" (be on lookout) for Garmel. I called police and introduced myself as Garmel's lawyer and I told them we would be surrendering soon. A Sergeant of the police fugitive squad told me it wasn't his leisure to sit back and wait for people accused of murder to turn themselves in at their leisure.

In the spirit of cooperation, I told them it would be soon. But, police already knew Garmel had returned to Jamaica and wanted a definite return date from me before the professional argument started. I don't think anyone likes to be threatened, especially not me, so I told him it would happen when it does. When Garmel returned a few days after my conversation with police, they snatched Garmel's ass off the plane, with news reporters in tow.

The case was assigned to old school Judge Barnes, who looked like he had just stepped out of the civil war. However, Judge Barnes liked to move his caseload, and Garmel's case was no exception. The method was that folks who were in jail trials would have priority over folks charged with crimes but were out on bond. I knew that after the District Attorney complained about Garmel fleeing to Jamaica that if he was released on bond, the old Judge Barnes was not going to give Garmel another chance to get lost. Bond was denied.

By the time we went to trial, I had a long list of witnesses the state was intending to call to testify about how Garmel stalked Vincente. Moreover, I knew they had found bits and pieces of Vincente's checkbook in Garmel's friend Lisa's fireplace. The problem was that Lisa didn't really know Vincente personally. So, why is Vincente's checkbook in her fireplace? Lisa was just a listening ear for Garmel, and she would just listen as Garmel complained about how Vincente treated him.

Garmel complained that when he would get to a point where he was almost over her, Vincente would reel him in again and allow him to taste her if she was just between boyfriends. Garmel bragged to me about the five abortions she had over the course of their relationship, as if that somehow diminished his blood sucking ways. Vincente's e-mails were downloaded by CSI and they showed Garmel referring to the "sucky-sucky" every time Vincente would allow him a taste.

When police questioned Lisa, she tried to protect Garmel's confidences as much as she could before police started suggesting that she was an accessory after the fact. Police claimed that Lisa knowingly allowed Garmel to burn Vincente's checkbook in her fireplace. Thereafter, Lisa started talking. Finally, Lisa allowed police to remove the ashes, which contained burnt pieces of Vincente's checkbook, from her fireplace.

At trial, I told Garmel he was not to mention anything about his kids he had out of wedlock. I especially told him not to mention anything about the five abortions. I thought Garmel and I were clear about what he was going to say and more importantly, what he wasn't going to say. I was wrong.

Seemingly, no sooner than I asked Garmel for his name, he told the jury about the three kids he has with his wife and the two younger kids he has with other women. Garmel followed that up with the five abortions he and Vincente had together. I guess Judge Barnes could tell by the look on my face that I felt a dick go up my ass. Not that I know how that feels, but you get my point.

Judge Barnes smacked his gavel and demanded both counsels to his chambers. When I got back there, his face was cherry red. He said, "Ted, I thought that you needed a break." Judge Barnes and I busted out laughing. I said to Judge Barnes, "I told that motherfucker not..." Judge Barnes interrupted me and said, "Ted, I know, I saw the look on your face."

The young prosecutor was just standing there dumbfounded. Obviously, he didn't know about the sport of law, and not to take this shit too seriously. Every time Judge Barnes and I thought we were composed enough to resume the trial, we'd bust out laughing again. For the remainder of the trial, Judge Barnes kept his head down like he was reading something, and I couldn't look at him because we knew we couldn't hold our laughter.

Officer Jones testified he had dated Vincente, but they were no more. On the night Vincente went missing, Officer Jones admitted he had in fact attempted to take Vincente her clothes, but she didn't open the door. He claimed he spoke to her by cell phone and they argued again. I told the jury that Officer Jones was the last person to see Vincente alive. I accused Officer Jones of her murder. He told the jury how Garmel approached him on his job about Vincente. Jones told them how he felt Garmel was unstable and capable of anything. He reasoned that Garmel approached him and he's licensed to carry a gun.

Officer Robinson testified about how he and Jones were patrol officers together and that Jones told him about his confrontation with Garmel. I asked Robinson if he considered Jones to be a friend. Robinson said that Jones was one of his best friends. I asked Robinson if he told Jones about the fact he tried to take Vincente out on a date. Much to Robinson's surprise, he only answered the question with, "No." Jones didn't know that Robinson was trying to creep with Vincente.

I looked at both Jones and Robinson like you fools know I have a stalker as a client, I know all about this shit. I asked Robinson if he would try to help Jones if he were in trouble with the law. Judge Barnes interrupted my question with a recess. While in the men's room, Jones and Robinson asked me to stop fucking with them. I did, I figured I made my point.

The business financier told the jury that Vincente was like a sister to him. Vincente was someone who he was going to mentor through the GMAT exam, and encouraged her to continue with her education. Mr. Financier didn't know I had the e-mails he had sent to Vincente telling her how nice and round her ass was. Financier also told her that he wanted to suck on her lips, and I reminded him that he didn't specify which set of lips he was talking about.

The financier forgot to tell the jury about the e-mails where he described Vincente's breast as perfect and how he wanted to touch them. But of course, I reminded him, and in some instances, I showed him the e-mails. Afterwards, I asked him if he had such conversations with his sister. Of course, Mr. Financier said, "No."

I also had him to admit that he was supposed to have met with Vincente for a run on the last day she was seen alive. I asked him if he had in fact seen her, and when he replied, No," I must admit,

I enjoyed how uncomfortable and defensive he had become as he testified. She was like a sister to me my ass.

The medical examiner testified about the putrid condition of Vincente's decomposing body in that hot apartment in July. The decomposition made it difficult to determine the time of her death, but the noodles found in her stomach gave them a ballpark estimate. The medical examiner then told the jury about her skin slippage and the stage of decomposition when that occurs. The DNA samples that were collected were unreliable due to the decomposition mixture that contaminated the samples. However, of what they could make of the DNA samples, Garmel couldn't be excluded as a suspect, and Jones could. The expert from the cell phone company placed Garmel's cell phone bouncing off of the cell tower near Vincente's apartment. As I recall, there was never any evidence presented on what cell phone tower Jones's phone was bouncing off. But, it didn't matter.

See, when the CSI experts flashed that infrared light into the checkbook ashes recovered from Lisa's fireplace, we were done. The jury found that it was Garmel who literally choked the shit out of Vincente, resulting in her death. However, they did not find him guilty of raping her. The underlying question remained the same throughout the trial, "Who lights a fireplace during Georgia's hot summer?" Lisa told the jury that Garmel lit her fireplace in July and we had no answer that made sense to rebut it.

After the trial, when I would see Judge Barnes, he would just say, "Ted, pick your face off the floor." Julie Brandau, the court reporter, would see me and say, "Ted! "sucky-sucky." It was our inside joke from Garmel's trial. In 2005, Judge Barnes was executed while presiding over a case in one the most horrific crimes in Atlanta history. The sexually abused murderer also killed Julie, a single mother, and Hoyt Teasley, a cop, husband, and father of three, who gave chase as the murderer fled from the courthouse. Officer Jones resigned from the Atlanta Police Department.

Sentence: Life in prison.

THOSE OF US

I remember one of the first things you learn as a child was that you never discussed family business outside of the house. The second thing was that you never talked about another black person in front of a non-black. Those of us who remember these days also remember that we lived in two worlds — one was black and the other was white. There was a time when I knew my brother, even though we were complete strangers, and I had only met him for the first time. We could have a full-blown conversation — everything said with our eyes.

We could converse with our sentiment of the moment, the cause and effect of those things around us. We could feel and understand the details of our circumstances and interpret them for life's sake and for laughs when we were alone. Those of us who remember, know that to be aloof was to place your life in jeopardy and that could get you killed. Today, these lessons have now become blurred, if not lost, in the newer generation. Sadly, some mistakenly think by their over use of the "N" word that it doesn't hurt as much as it used to. Like when niggas evolved to the more dignified Negro, before taking on the name of a haircut, Afro-American. Then we were black, and eventually we began calling ourselves African-American. Seemingly everything has gone full-circle.

Ms. Irene was one of us who balanced her life to fit into the other world. She enjoyed going to the theater and the company Christmas party. She enjoyed selling soda and candy out of her apartment to the ghetto kids in her neighborhood so she could buy that festive dress she saw in the window at Macy's. Ms. Irene knew how important it was to fit into the other world. Most of us still know how to dummy ourselves down to lessen the appearance of a threat, or how to be a strong black man. Those of us who remember these days knew that at the end of the day, we needed the check that came along with the self-deprecation and humiliation.

Even though Ms. Irene knew how to survive in her world and theirs, no one showed up for her trial. They covered her murder trial on the six o'clock news, but I expected that more of them would show an interest, since she did at one time work for them at the station as their receptionist. During the trial, only one black female showed up to support Ms. Irene's only daughter. After all, Ms. Irene did fit in without becoming an Uncle Tom which is a dreadful accusation made against many blacks who learn how to assimilate into the other world, their world, the white one. However, Ms. Irene's 18-year-old murder case was just the lead story on the six o'clock news, where she worked.

John Caldwell was accused of killing Ms. Irene. Caldwell was a man who lived in the same ghetto where Ms. Irene lived. He would see her day in and day out, dressed to the nines, going to work at the news station. Ms. Irene's job gave her prestige in the community. For little girls, she was someone to look up to because she was a point of reference, an example you can live in two worlds because everybody knew she worked with them but she lived with us. Ms. Irene was special to a lot of people in her community.

As we prepared to represent Caldwell, I learned many things about Ms. Irene. It's not unusual for an attorney to divert the attention away from his client and blame the victim for her own death. As silly as it sounds, it's not uncommon to hear a fool say that she was asking to be raped because of the clothes that she wore.

Attorney Dave Dunlap was fresh out of law school and lived a rather privileged life. I viewed him as just another bushy-tailed liberal trying to see if he was cut out for this cops and robbers shit that I called my practice. Dunlap seemed to have lived a good life and, based on his privileged life, he had many options and was optimistic about his life. Although Dunlap was my help, there were many things that I cared not to share with him about my culture, but I did anyway.

Ms. Irene was good at balancing her life in two worlds, but she was lonely. She loved the people in her community, but she knew that she couldn't take them anywhere. At the time of her death, Ms. Irene was dating a married jheri-curl-wearing man named Herman. She complained to Ms. Nancy, a neighbor, that she would take to the theater every now and then, when the station gave her comp tickets to plays nobody wanted to see. Ms. Irene complained to Ms. Nancy of how she was tired of fucking Herman because of his dirty, greasy-ass mechanic hands. The smell of his jheri-curl nauseated her and left grease stains on her sofa and bed, when she found herself horny enough to give in.

Caldwell knew Ms. Irene well and he knew where she worked. Being the career criminal that he was, he knew she would never give him a shot. At least the mechanic had a dream of owning his own shop, leaving his wife, and being with her. At least that was the dream he sold her. Caldwell would watch Ms. Irene go to and from work. He saw that she had style and dressed classy. He often fantasized about her.

When Ms. Irene didn't report for work on Monday and Tuesday, her daughter received a call from the station about her absence. Her daughter wasted no time in driving over to Ms. Irene's apartment and using her key to enter. She found her mother dead. When police arrived, they found Ms. Irene with her hands tied behind her back and her feet tied up with her hands. Ms. Irene was hogtied and she was naked. Her multi-colored headscarf was tied around her neck and was used to cover her nose and mouth.

At the time of her death, there were no witnesses to her murder. Ms. Irene's lover had an alibi and there were no other suspects. The only physical evidence the police could use to link to a suspect was a shoe print. When the case went cold, Caldwell had been arrested for a couple of unrelated burglaries and was sent to prison. Before Caldwell was released from prison, The Department of Corrections took a sample of his spit to store in the DNA storage bank for future use. At the time, DNA was a new science that hadn't been mastered, but was on its way to change forensic science forever.

It took the State of Georgia several years to fund the testing of DNA samples against the samples collected in cases of murder and rape, where the investigations have gone cold. After they ran random samples that included Caldwell's stuff, the police retested their evidence against Caldwell and it was a hit (or match) in the evidence collected and tested in Ms. Irene's case.

The first mistake that Caldwell made was that Caldwell had told police he didn't know Ms. Irene. As far as police are concerned, if you don't know her, how can your sperm be found in her body? The second mistake made was that Caldwell told police he didn't know how his sperm got inside of Ms. Irene's body. Police replied, "Well, either you put it there or your identical twin put it there." Caldwell told police that he didn't have a twin.

Police arrested Caldwell. I remember watching it on the six o'clock news. It was merely ironic that I faithfully watched the news on the same station where Ms. Irene had worked. When Caldwell was told he would be charged with Ms. Irene's murder, he faked a heart attack. I said to myself, "Look at his ass stretched out on the stretcher." I said to myself, "Get your chummy ass up and walk!" Little did I know that Caldwell would end up being my client. Little did I know that I would have the dubious distinction of trying one of the first cold cases in the history of Atlanta criminal justice.

When I first met Caldwell, he told me he didn't know Ms. Irene and that he would just see her in the neighborhood. After I explained to him about the DNA and how it works, Caldwell told me he and Irene had a sexual relationship, but it was on the down low. I didn't like the fact that Caldwell initially lied to me, but I was used to it and somewhat expected it. At least Caldwell has now provided me with an explanation of how his sperm got inside Ms. Irene.

There was nothing special about the trial. The experts all testified about how Caldwell's DNA was found in Ms. Irene's body. The police testified about how Caldwell lied about even knowing Ms. Irene. But, no one was ready for what I was about to do and that was to explain black culture or idiom to folks who were non-black. I was about to break the rules I was taught not to do as a boy. I was going to explain what it means to be on the down low.

The term "down low" is an expression used in black culture that has been around since the days of slavery, when one slave would teach another to read. House slaves would try to show favor to the field slaves in ways that needed to be kept secret because the penalty if you were caught was a whipping, lynching, or sometimes death. Sadly, the term "down low" was used to secret information from other blacks because they would tell on each other to get favor with the master.

Today, gay men who are still in the closet largely use the term "down low" in an effort to secret their homosexuality. In the gay community, when married men have sexual relationships with gay men, it is considered to be a relationship on the down low. Conversely, in heterosexual relationships, the term "down low" is used by couples that secret their relationships or by married men who cheat on their wives with other women.

Caldwell's theory was that he had a sexual relationship with Ms. Irene because her neighbors knew of her relationship with Herman. Besides, she didn't want her neighbors to know that she was dating beneath her with the likes of Caldwell. Ms. Irene lived in two worlds and Caldwell didn't fit into her public life, but did have a place in her private one.

Although I believe that the jury had some appreciation for my history lesson on black folks, the jury found the place where my theory had come from as it related to Caldwell and put it back in my ass as easily as I had pulled it out.

The jury didn't care about the fact there were no witnesses who saw Caldwell near or around Ms. Irene's house prior to the murder. Caldwell didn't help the situation. When he admitted he had worked on the property where Ms. Irene lived, replacing the windows. Detectives had surmised that the offender had entered through Ms. Irene's window. A size 12 shoe print was found on top of Ms. Irene's stereo set, which was placed right underneath the window. Caldwell wore a size 12 shoe.

The medical examiner testified that Ms. Irene Hyoid Bone had been crushed. He described it as that little fragile bone near or around your windpipes in your neck that helps you breathe. The headscarf around her neck and mouth was tied too tight and resulted in her death. Ms. Irene didn't die immediately. The terror of it all is that she knew she was suffocating and she couldn't do anything about it.

I gave Caldwell the best defense I had in my bag of tricks and he thanked me. After the medical examiner explained how the scarf was tied too tight, I knew he didn't try to kill her, but it didn't make me feel any better. To the contrary, I was ashamed of myself for telling some folks about those of us.

Sentence: Life in prison.

Chapter 6

Revenge

PIG

Regina was just a single mother with two kids. Her mother was a bus driver for a bus line and her father was a retired factory worker. Like most single mothers, Regina would date men she believed would accept her boys. But, more often than not, she knew she had to pay them from time to time when she got her check. That was okay with her as long as they treated her boys okay and the dick was good and available when she wanted it. For the most part, Regina treated her men like one of her children because she was usually the breadwinner.

When I met Regina, she was serving life in prison for murder. From the photos I had seen of her from the trial, Regina was tall and skinny. But, in person, Regina had gained weight. She was tall, wore glasses, and had a little acne on her face. To look at her, you would find her to be sort of homely looking, but she wasn't. Regina was an around-the-way girl who didn't look for shit, but wasn't 'gone take any shit either.

I informed Regina that her father hired me to represent her. Regina asked me if I could help her. She told me she could live with the fact that she would never see her boys again on the outside, but she couldn't take knowing that her mother would spend the rest of her life in prison because of her. Regina wanted me to do anything I could to help her mother. Seemingly, Regina had resigned herself to serve the rest of her life in prison.

Regina didn't know she was talking to a flirt, a man who happened to be a lawyer that had a soft spot for women as much as he had a hard one. Although I wasn't attracted to Regina, I flirted with her anyway because that's what flirts do. I just wanted Regina to remember what it was like to feel like a woman. I assumed for no other reason that she didn't feel like a woman because she was in jail. A flirt's way of a random act of kindness, I felt sorry for her. Regina flirted back. I think it was as amusing for her as it was for me.

Regina told me she was just a working girl and that she never had a job that paid a lot of money. She'd work from factory to factory and from one fast food joint to the next. Regina shared that she really never had shit, but what she did have, she earned. Regina lived in Southeast Atlanta, in a crime-ridden area where crack cocaine had taken over her neighborhood. Regina told me how she would see crackheads just walking up and down the street all day. They had no job and no destination in sight. They were just on the move.

Regina said she would change her locks every time someone would break into her home. But, after awhile, she decided that it didn't matter which locks she'd put on her door, they would find another way to get into her home. Regina's house had been burglarized three times in three weeks. After each burglary, she would ask her neighbors if they saw anyone around her house while she was at work. Each time, they would tell her no.

Pig was in his mid to late twenties. he was a high school dropout and a crackhead. Homeless, people allowed him to crash at their place. Regina never told me about the neighbors who allowed Pig to crash at their place. We never got past Pig in her conversation.

Regina told me that she never intended to kill Pig, but it was just as much his fault as it was hers. She insisted her mother had nothing to do with it.

Regina received a call at work from a neighbor informing her that her home had been burglarized. When she got home, she didn't know whether they kicked her door in again or busted out a window. It really didn't matter. The neighbors, she guessed, were just as tired of her home being burglarized as she was. They told her who the culprit was. They told her it was Pig.

Regina called the police and made a report. Regina then called her mother and told her about the break-in and that she had learned it was Pig. Regina told me she had known Pig from the community. She knew Pig as one of the crackheads that just hung out in the area and occasionally slept next door.

Regina said she had purchased a gun from a pawnshop for protection, after she was burglarized the first time. She hid the gun in her home, away from her kids. After she learned that it was nasty-ass Pig who kept breaking into her home, she got her gun and got into the car with her mother. One of her neighbors told Regina that Pig was over at the liquor store off Ashby Street. When Regina and her mother arrived, Pig had already left for Adair Park with some people in a pickup truck. As Regina and her mother pulled into the park, they observed Pig sitting in the back of a pickup truck.

As Regina got out of the car, she approached the truck and started talking to Pig. Regina told me that Pig had a smirk on his face like, "What does this bitch want?" Regina noticed that the other guys in the truck were also laughing as if she was Pig's woman demanding that he come home for dinner or something. "Pig, why do you keep breaking into my home?" Regina asked. "Cause I can," said Pig. Regina said that's when she lost it and pulled out her gun.

The guys sitting in the back of the truck jumped out, trying to get away from Regina. Regina's mother picked up a stick as soon as they pulled up to the area where Pig was. After Pig called himself getting smart, Regina's mother threw the stick at him. After her mother threw the stick at Pig, Regina said she thought Pig was jumping out of the truck to get her. So she fired her gun. As soon as she fired the gun, the guy pulled off in the truck, forcing Pig to fall over the side. The truck then rolled over Pig and broke his leg. Regina shot Pig in the stomach. Pig died on the way to the hospital.

Regina and her mother were charged with the murder of Pig. Regina's father went out and hired the attorney that handled his social security benefits claims. The attorney practiced law for over 15 years, but he never handled a murder case before. The benefits lawyer sought out a friend who was also a civil attorney who practiced criminal law off and on for a while, but hadn't tried a murder case in a number of years. Feeling confident, Regina's mother would wear her bus uniform to trial every day. Seemingly, who would convict her for throwing a stick at a dirty ass Pig?

The state talked about how Regina and her mother drove around town like two mad women looking for a Pig to kill. Regina's attorneys tried to show that Pig had a violent criminal history and Regina had reason to be afraid of him. In their incompetence, her attorneys failed to properly call the appropriate witnesses, so the court refused to allow the jury to hear about Pig's violent past.

Even more, Regina and her mother were never told by their attorneys that the state was offering Regina a plea-bargain that would have her serve only 10 years in prison and allow her mother to walk away scot-free. As a result of the lack of information, Regina and her mom were convicted of murder and sentenced to life in prison.

Judge Diane Smith Henry Williams affectionately referred to as the Diva. She presided over Regina's trial. Judge Diva would often joke about her name, but still respected the men in her life, past and present. Jokingly, Diva would say with her English accent, *"I shall resign if I ever marry again because my name would not fit on the marquee."* If she didn't respect an attorney who shared any of her names, she would tell the audience that the attorney was of no relation to her.

Judge Henry-Williams: "Is attorney Williams present? Attorney Williams, please reply Attorney Williams."

"I'm here, Judge."

Judge Henry-Williams would then look at the attorney and look away into the audience of court spectators and say, "No relation."

At least for me, it was always funny as hell. A living legend, Diva was the first African-American Chief Judge in Atlanta Superior Court History.

Judge Henry-Williams was affectionately referred to as the "Diva" because of her pomp and circumstance. Diva was a pioneer in Atlanta in all circles: LPH (long, pretty hair), full makeup and expensive perfumes were her thing. But Diva was probably one of the most patient and smartest people I have ever met. She was certainly smarter than me. Diva once told me that I irritated her and I got on her last nerve. She said she couldn't take me. But, Lord forbid, if she ever got in to trouble with the law, I would be her first phone call. At first, I didn't believe her because of the sheer number of top-flight attorneys in Atlanta. However, the Diva's assistant of many years told me that the Diva meant what she said.

On appeal, I was able to bring the case back to the Diva. I knew that I was about to ask the Diva to do something she had done only one other time in her 30-year career — reverse the jury's verdict. I told the Diva how sorry and with ill-prepared the attorneys were that represented Regina and her mother. I explained how they failed to secure proper witnesses and their misplaced belief that they could just present an affidavit in exchange for witness testimony and how this reflected their incompetence. The attorneys confessed they never told Regina or her mother that the state would dismiss charges against her mom if Regina had accepted 10 years in prison as a plea bargain. This was yet another travesty. When I confronted the attorney about why he failed to communicate the plea bargain to Regina, he simply told me that he thought he could win her case. Instead, Regina and her mother were sentenced to life in prison because of his arrogance.

It took me close to five years, but in 2004, the Diva reversed Regina's conviction. The District Attorney then allowed Regina to plead guilty to a 10-year sentence. Regina was released on parole in 2007. As a result of Regina's plea bargain, in 2004, her mother was immediately released from prison. Sadly, she died of cirrhosis of the liver in 2008. In 2009, the Diva remarried and resigned from the bench.

JUNETEENTH

I thought it odd in the beginning that one brother was named Elroy Flowers and the other named Virgil Withers. As it turned out, Virgil was trying to permanently wither Elroy's flowers from this life to the grave. It is a story of two teenagers feuding over a gun, and one figured the other must die. Thus, it came to pass on a Juneteenth Day in the year of the 1996 Olympic Games in Atlanta.

Demario was gunned down. He was shot in the neck outside of Elroy's apartment on a day over 200 years ago, when Lincoln freed the slaves. Somehow, the slaves in Texas didn't get the fax that Lincoln sent word they were free. So they remained in slavery an extra two years. As it is, many young black men are still enslaved over 200 years later. They're enslaved by crime, prison, disease, and educational ignorance.

Names like Virgil and Elroy couldn't possibly be more English. Both men were born in the 1970's and you would think their names would be Khalil or Jamal or some other made-up name like Sertonious, DeQuan or even Tyrone. But Virgil and Elroy from the projects of Atlanta.

Some people ask, "What's in a name?" They say the person makes the name and not the other way around. There may be some truth to that notion. However, I think your name is your first impression. The second impression is when people actually meet you. In America, it matters if your last name is Hatfield or McCoy; Kennedy or Cosby; Reagan or Poitier; Clinton or King. In America, we associate names with wealth and status.

You'd think that as teenagers, Elroy and Virgil's only real purpose in life was to finish high school or chase little girls. Instead, Elroy and Virgil fought over a .25 mm automatic handgun. I don't think there was anything special or unique about the gun. No famous crook like Bumpy, of Harlem, or Dillinger, of Indiana, had owned the .25 mm automatic. It was just a cheap gun that 15-year-old Virgil allowed 16-year-old Elroy to observe. Somewhere, in between the shit talking and threats, Elroy beat Virgil's ass and kept his gun.

Like most men, it's not the fact that you got your ass whipped, it's the fact that someone saw you get your ass whipped. To these few, you must do something that would trump the ass whipping. You must do something to restore your manhood. If you failed to do this, then you were considered soft and unworthy. Your reputation was attacked and your street credibility — if you had any in the first place — is gone. To those who matter, you must provide evidence that you have redeemed yourself from the ass whipping. Even if the friendship isn't that important to you, walking away isn't an option.

Unfortunately and all too often, the provocation for murder was simply stepping on someone's shoe or laughing at a joke directed at another. "Why are you laughing? You don't know me like that!" is all the provocation that's needed.

A year after Virgil got his ass whipped by Elroy, they met by chance at a traffic light. Virgil immediately recognized Elroy in the next car. Virgil was in the front passenger seat of the other car. Virgil challenged Elroy to meet him in a park around the corner. I suppose Virgil would have shot Elroy in the park if he were stupid enough to go. Elroy knew better. As the light turned green, Elroy and Virgil drag raced down Ashby Street. Elroy was able to bump Virgil's car just enough to change lanes and turn off at the intersection on Martin Luther King Boulevard. Virgil's car, unable to turn off, kept straight. Virgil, sitting on the passenger door, with half his body out of the car, began to scream at Elroy, "What's up nigga? I'll see you again."

True to his word, Virgil found out Elroy was living in the Harris Homes Housing Projects. In broad daylight in March 1996, Virgil pulled up to Elroy's apartment, which he shared with his mother, brothers, and sister, and opened fire. Virgil fired several rounds from a 9 mm at Elroy. What bothered me most was that Elroy's mother and 12-year-old sister had to run and duck for cover. They were all in the line of fire, but Virgil didn't care. As the shots rang out, everyone scattered. Virgil hopped back into his car and fled. I guess technically, this was not a drive-by shooting, since Virgil stood outside the car when he fired the gun. At the time of the shooting, Virgil was only 17 years old and Elroy was now 18 years old.

I was angry with Elroy's mother for not calling the police and not giving them a report after this occurred. I know I represented Withers, but I still care if future crimes can be prevented with a phone call. Unfortunately, sometimes nothing is done to help the police. Sadly, people sometimes do nothing to help themselves. I soon figured out that Elroy's mother had no control over Elroy or his brother, just as Virgil's mother had no control over him. I guess Elroy and Virgil's mothers were just teenagers themselves when they began having children. Elroy and Virgil were babies that grew up with their parents.

Eventually, momma met another man and here comes another baby's daddy. The cycle continues until kid number four or five. Both of my sisters stopped at kid number three. However, one sister had a child who died as a baby. I can proudly say that her two surviving children went on to become college graduates. My oldest sister has two daughters with some college courses behind them.

However, her 30-year-old high school dropout, crack-using son still lives with her, carrying unresolved issues from childhood. Today, he claims to be preacher. But I can look at him and tell he's still using. I say that to say there are some exceptions.

I'm not supposed to know how Virgil felt when he met the father of his little sister and then his baby brother, even though he knew that he and his older brother had the same father. I don't doubt that Virgil loved his brothers and sister, as I love my own, but I never saw my mother with another man. The effect this may have on my young psyche is unknown to me. However, this effect may be very real to Virgil and perhaps Elroy.

I'm pretty confident, even if I'm making an assumption, that neither Virgil nor Elroy had any idea of what Juneteenth Day is, or what it means. They may have heard of President Lincoln only because they were force-fed the information in school. Like most kids, both Virgil and Elroy started out as emptied vessels. They're anxious to be fed knowledge by a parent and eager to be approved in the eyes of the world. But they got lost. They got lost in circumstances beyond their control. By the time they were 10 years old, they were unparentable and contemptuous because the one authority figure in their life — their mother — was constantly compromising their needs for her own needs — and for her desire to be loved by a man.

The neglect ran deep in Virgil and Elroy's veins, and they remember the pain, shame, and embarrassment momma brought them. They remember how it felt the first time momma chose a man over them. Eventually, they expected momma to choose them second. The pain, like anything else, doesn't hurt as much as it used to — not like the first time. The pain lessens as they come to terms with their reality. At some point, the pain becomes hidden by false bravado and bitterness. Respect for authority was lost because they didn't even respect their own mommas. Confused by this maternal love thing, they learned to cope and rationalize as young, angry black men.

Confused, frustrated, and impatient by the absence of maternal love, the act of love has trickled down to just an act, thing, or status. The whole dissociative behavioral attitude of those he was supposed to love is now objectified by the impersonal "my baby momma." Even worse, society has placed these young men together in an environment where this phenomenon occurs more often than not — the projects. Yet, we are surprised and dismayed when these young men wear their pants beneath their ass. Seemingly, the projects are a project that has failed the black family.

On June 19, 1996, Demario Williams was standing outside of Elroy's apartment. It was dark outside, but Elroy was trying to work on his car. Elroy eventually gave up on any more work that night and returned a flashlight to the apartment. Then the shots rang out and Demario was hit. He fell right in front of Elroy's apartment door. Seemingly, he was running to get inside of the house. Elroy knew it had to be Virgil. Virgil shot Demario, thinking it was Elroy. Demario was only 18 years old himself.

Before Elroy called the police, he got his 9 mm and began firing in the direction of the car Virgil was in. Elroy told police it was Virgil who killed Demario. However, no witnesses could identify Virgil as the shooter. Later Elroy claimed he recognized Virgil's voice.

At the time of the shooting, Elroy claimed the shooter yelled out his name, "Yeah, yeah Elroy." Elroy, said when he heard the voice, he knew it to be Virgil's. Elroy told police that he recognized the voice because he and Virgil went to elementary school together. At trial, it was learned that Elroy's mother didn't know he and his older brother owned guns and kept them in the house. Apparently, at 18 years of age, Elroy had no hesitation to own a gun and keep it in his mother's house.

Ten days later, Virgil was riding as a passenger in a stolen car when it was pulled over by police. Police recovered the murder weapon from the car. Other passengers told police that the gun belonged to Virgil. Virgil, still 17 years old, was riding with another male teenager and two 29-year-old women. They were about to steal a swim at an apartment complex in a neighboring county. I guess Virgil didn't have time for women his own age.

I just couldn't believe Virgil would be stupid enough to be riding around with the murder weapon in a stolen car. Virgil even had a bag of ammunition on him when he was arrested. But, hey, teenagers do stupid shit. At least the bullets police recovered from him didn't match the bullets that killed Demario.

As it was, the murder weapon and the voice identification of Virgil was enough to convict Virgil of murder. I convinced Virgil not to testify on his own behalf. I figured I could win without him having to explain the shooting that occurred in broad daylight a few months before the murder. Plus, I felt Virgil was too ignorant to help himself. I guess I either figured wrong or the jury just wasn't buying my bullshit that day.

On a Juneteenth Day during Atlanta's first and only Olympics, it was a humid 95 degrees with clear skies. It was a day of historical significance for many reasons.

However, for Virgil and Elroy, it was the day Demario was killed. Sadly, Virgil, Elroy, or most of their generation will never fully understand the concept of sacrificing for their freedom. However, for Elroy and Virgil, we still hope that through life experiences, they will learn. We hope they learn the challenges and sacrifices they must make for their own freedom and the freedom they have taken for granted for too long.

Demario will never know what freedom is like here on earth. But, perhaps, Demario is now free — especially if his life was anything like Elroy or Virgil's. However, I do know that no one had the right to take Demario's hope of finding his own journey to freedom. That is what's so regretful.

Sentence: Virgil Withers life in prison.

PRECIOUS

I thought about my life again today and asked myself the same question. Is it worth it? June told me she loved me today the best way that she could. I know that June is trapped in her world. In the past, June believed she had already given those she loved too much. And, given what June's been through, no one can really argue with her. June told me that when it comes to men, she's always paid too much for what she got in return. Not many of us will go to prison for 15 years out of our love for another. But now, June has a child. And that keeps her honest.

June was sentenced to over 15 years of federal time because she wouldn't tell. She didn't want to be a snitch and tell on her lover. June was only 19 at best when they sent her down the river for nearly 20 years. Today, she will tell you if she had to do it all over again, she wouldn't. I love her because she did it the first time. I love her because after she did it, she finished college and then law school. I love June because she had a commitment I've longed for but never had — to protect her so-called lover, however misplaced her love was. Again, I was asked how I do this shit every day. And, again, it hurts. However rhetorical the question, it hurts. But I'm too much of a coward to do something else.

Precious was killed on the morning of July 27. She was only nine years old. She was sitting at her computer when a stray bullet fatally struck her in the head. There she was, head slouched over her keyboard, arms extended like a small bird. From across the room, the cartoon network was blaring from the television. My heart cried. I tried to avoid looking at her crime scene pictures, but I somehow mishandled her file and I saw them. I saw Precious slouched over and my heart cried.

June told me she didn't want to read any of my stories that dealt with the death of a child, and I obliged her. She had her own daughter to think of and the death of another child was too much for her to find interest in. But today, I needed her help. I needed her to tell me it was all right to represent the fucker who killed Precious. I've never needed June's permission on any case I was working on. But on this morning, I wanted to just hear her voice. I know that God has given me much in my life. I can honestly say that I can't ever thank God for what he's already done. But, if God were to appear right now and ask me if I needed anything, I would always be able to ask for just one more thing.

But with June, I know that she has already given a lot to others, and that can't be replaced. As much as I love her, I just can't ask her for anything or go against her wishes. I don't think I deserve to expect anything from June, but I do. I knew in reading everything I could about Precious, like June, she had an appreciation for knowledge. Like June, Precious had a love of life, a passion inside of her that I couldn't imagine but wanted to embrace, a life anyone would want to make better. Sadly, like June, the people she loved the most failed her in their indecision.

As I walked into the courtroom, the news reporters were there with their cameras posted up against the wall pointing at Ardeaux and his co-defendant, Melvin Jones. Ardeaux moved here as a result of hurricane Katrina, along with many others. I tried to find out something about Ardeaux that I liked, but there was nothing. Ardeaux was selfish, self-centered, and had a one-track mind. He was all about himself. I just wanted the brother to say, "Ted, you know I didn't mean to do this." To the contrary, Ardeaux was comfortable with the notion that I already knew of his empathy without him saying it. Nonetheless, I wanted to hear it — remorse is what it's called — and Ardeaux never showed me any — nor did he give any to Precious. Nigga.

We struck a jury in one day, which was pretty good considering there were two defendants at the table charged with Precious' murder. It usually takes me a day by myself. At a recess, Precious' mother, Wanda, walked her retarded self out of the courtroom. Wanda walked with a limp, and was basically a happy person. Wanda was aware of what was happening. It just took her longer to process stuff. As Wanda glanced out, she looked at me and smiled. I was returning from the men's room. In an instance, she looked at me again and began to cry. In her retardation, she understood that her nine-year-old Precious was dead. She understood I was the fucker who represented the killer, and I was trying to get him off. Through her tears, she smiled at me again. She made me feel ashamed of myself.

Until that experience, I never imagined I would ever care about what anyone thought of me. Sure, I care about those I love and what they think of me, but a retarded stranger? I can't say that I have ever given it any thought. Again, I feel God is reeling me in from the darkness I call my job. At that moment, I really needed to speak to June about my feelings for her, but I couldn't call her without talking about Precious, so I decided not to call.

From a professional standpoint, there was nothing special about Ardeaux's case. He and Jones drove over to Tiny Man's marijuana trap to rob him. At the time, Ardeaux was broke and he was being evicted from the rental house he shared with his girlfriend, Sheila. Sheila was a pregnant stripper with one child and another on the way. So, Sheila was broke, too. On July 27, three years after hurricane Katrina, Ardeaux and Jones drove over to Tiny's place and waved him down. Tiny, who also held a 9 to 5 at UPS, had a rule when it came to selling his weed. Tiny didn't sell to people he didn't know. After Tiny approached Ardeaux's car, he refused to sell to Ardeaux. Ardeaux grabbed Tiny by his collar and began to spray bullets in his direction. Tiny fell to the ground, but was able to get back on his feet and run away in a full zig-zag sprint. The bullet intended for Tiny traveled through Precious' bedroom window, striking her in the head.

The night before her death, Precious received a new laptop for her birthday. They say she couldn't wait to get up the next morning to play with it. That morning, Precious got up from her bed and turned on her television. She made her bed, then went to the bathroom and dressed herself. Precious then went to the kitchen, where she ate some cereal. After she finished her cereal, Precious returned to her bedroom and sat on a stool in front of a built-in bookcase that she used as a desk. Precious never had a chance to turn her computer on before she was killed.

Precious, an ambitious honor student, lived with her grandmother, who I think was originally from the Washington, DC area. Precious liked school and riding her bike. When her grandmother wouldn't let her go outside, she would play school with her brother. She was frequently barred from going outside because of the dope boys who took over the apartment complex where Precious lived. Grandma, on most days, didn't want to stay outside and watch them play because she worked all day. Precious could only go outside if grandma was watching.

As conflicted as I was about Ardeaux, it didn't take long for the bitch to come out of me. I was shitty with Ardeaux and Tiny. I was shitty with all the witnesses who came to testify about what they saw, and I was shitty with Grandma. Of all the people who lived in this apartment complex and knew Tiny sold drugs right in front of Precious' window, no one ever called police on Tiny. This ghetto attitude of, "If I can just mind my own business, somehow shit will stop, or crime will go away," is detrimental because shit never just goes away. Someone has to shovel it.

I was shitty with Tiny because he sold drugs out of his momma's house and did so around kids. People even said that Tiny's mother sold marijuana. Now Precious is dead and everyone wants to come to court and cry about it. Who are the tears really for? Precious? Or are they tears of guilt because nothing was done to protect her? Are you just sad that she's dead? I guess it's never too late to cry. Just don't cry to impress me.

I confronted Precious' grandmother about her reluctance to call the police. She told me she confronted Tiny about selling his drugs in front of her apartment. She seemed proud of the fact that Tiny's crew considered her 'the mean lady' and wouldn't sell around her. However, she would see the crew disperse from around her apartment every time she returned home from work. But, Tiny's drug deals were none of her business, as long as he didn't sell it around her. The bottom line is she never called police. To me, grandma was just as guilty by doing nothing to protect Precious and all the kids of the complex. She allowed the dope boys to take over her community. To me, she was a coward.

The witnesses presented by the state identified the car Ardeaux was driving. Within an hour of the shooting, police stopped Ardeaux's girlfriend, Sheila, at a nearby drugstore. During the stop, police observed a pregnant Sheila with a new prescription of prenatal vitamins. Unsure about the car, they took her name and address before they released her.

I remembered watching the outcry of Precious' death on the evening news. The newsman advised viewers to "be on lookout for two black males wearing baseball caps driving a black Chevy with a red drive-out tag." I recalled saying that could be anyone, but it wasn't.

Ardeaux knew he was hot and he was looking to get out of town, so he called his cousin Benny. Benny was a career thief and a convicted liar. Ardeaux told Benny what had occurred and asked for money. And Benny gave it to him. He placed $500 in the mailbox of the rental property where Ardeaux lived and called him to retrieve it before the mailman came. Benny then arranged for a group of his girlfriends to place anonymous calls to the police, implicating Ardeaux. The police followed up on the information Benny provided and issued a warrant for Ardeaux's arrest.

At trial, police testified to all of this and admitted to lying to Jones so he would implicate Ardeaux. Police then lied to Ardeaux so he would to implicate Jones. Ardeaux never told on Jones. However, Sheila told police that Ardeaux did own a small silver gun and a big black gun. Moreover, she hadn't seen the silver gun in a while. Sheila also told police that Jones and Ardeaux were together at the house on the morning of Precious' death. This was a small detail that Ardeaux forgot to tell police when they questioned him. In fact, Ardeaux told police he didn't even know Jones, even after they showed him Jones' picture.

Sheila tried to change her statement to police and explained to the jury that the silver gun was hers, but she either misplaced it or someone had stolen it along with her purse. Witnesses at the scene stated the shooter had a silver gun that resembled a 9 mm.

Benny got on the witness stand and told his story. Benny told the jury he is 30 years old and still lives with his mother. Of course I knew better. Benny was still hustling. He admitted to having female friends place the anonymous calls to police regarding Precious' murder. Like Lil Wayne, one of Benny's women worked in law enforcement. In the past, Benny even admitted he had given police about 20 fake names he used in his criminal days. But, the fact I'm bringing that shit up now has nothing to do with Ardeaux killing Precious. Police even told the jury that Benny refused to take the reward money. He instructed police to give the money to Precious' family.

Ardeaux basically denied being at the apartment complex and shooting at anyone. Ardeaux stated Benny was lying because a few weeks ago he had to pistol-whip Benny over some money. Benny's head had to be stapled back together.

Ardeaux was convicted of murder and Jones, who sat quietly throughout the trial, was found not guilty on all counts. The jury convicted Ardeaux even though they didn't know about the murder case he had pending in New Orleans. Tiny didn't testify at the trial. A stray bullet in an unrelated drug transaction killed him. Tiny's mother is convinced that a fellow neighbor, an old lady and evacuee from New Orleans, placed a voodoo spell on Tiny. I'll tell you, God is something else. The day after the trial, I talked to June all day. I told her, "June, I love you baby." June replied, "Thanks, but I ain't trying to hear all of that. Can you just meet me for a glass of wine?"

Sentence: Ardeaux life plus twenty years.

FACES I HAVE SEEN

Ted Johnson

ABOUT THE AUTHOR

Ted Johnson has a successful career as a criminal defense lawyer and is originally from Indianapolis, Ind. He attended Rice University and Thurgood Marshall School of Law, before moving to Chicago in 1989. He then trained as a prosecutor in the Cook County State Attorney's Office before moving to Atlanta, Ga., in 1993. In Atlanta, he began his criminal defense career and became a public defender. In 1996, he started his law firm and entered into private practice. He still resides in the Atlanta area.